IRON IN THE BLOOD

Thames Ironworks FC, the club that became West Ham United

John Powles

A *SoccerData* Publication from Tony Brown

Published in Great Britain by Tony Brown,
4 Adrian Close, Beeston, Nottingham NG9 6FL.
Telephone 0115 973 6086. E-mail soccer@innotts.co.uk
First published 2005

The author was born and bred in West Ham and attended the local Plaistow
Grammar School. He saw his first match at Upton Park at the age of eight in 1943
and has been a season-ticket holder at West Ham United for many years.

ACKNOWLEDGEMENTS

I would first like to thank Tony Brown for giving me the encouragement to complete
this book and for its subsequent publication. Special thanks go to Stuart Allen who
provided invaluable assistance regarding a number of unrecorded player appearances
and goalscorers which resolved a number of mysteries and helped to give the first
detailed and comprehensive statistical playing record of Thames Ironworks FC,
although it is disappointing that after very extensive research a small number of the
earliest records appear to be irretrievable. I would also like to thank John Northcutt
for his advice and I am also indebted to my friends Dennis Chamberlain and Jim
Glover who gave me help of a technical nature.
        Thanks should also go to staff at the Newspaper Library at Colindale and
particularly to those at the Newham Local Studies Library at Stratford, East London.
Photographs of Thames Ironworks and its products are the copyright of Newham
Archives and Local Studies Library and are reproduced with their kind permission.

John Powles, April 2005

ISBN 1 899468 22 6
Printed by 4Edge, Hockley, Essex

Contents

Many famous football clubs can trace their origins from humble beginnings in the latter part of the 19th Century, with a number rising from the background of the smoke and grime of industrial England. One such club is West Ham United, born out of, and owing its existence to Thames Ironworks FC, a shipbuilding company club founded in the final years of the Victorian age. The aim of this book is to explain something of the history surrounding the original club's foundation, to record the triumphs and failures in its short existence, and to describe the problems subsequently encountered when the decision was made to make the transition from amateur status, when the players involved kicked the ball about more from the relief of their daily grind, and to enjoy the game for its own sake, to that of a purely professional organisation when the club's balance sheet took on greater importance, and players joined the club more from a mercenary viewpoint than playing purely for pleasure.

    A thumbnail history of Thames Ironworks & Shipbuilding Company is covered in the introduction, along with a profile of Mr Arnold Hills, the Chairman and Managing Director of the company, who was the central figure in the financing and consolidation of the football club and instrumental in its progression to West Ham United.

INTRODUCTION

Shipbuilding along the banks of the Thames had been carried out since the sixteenth century but the story here begins in 1837 at the onset of the Victorian age, when C. J. Mare, already a shipbuilder at the age of twenty three, went into partnership with Thomas Ditchburn, who had served his apprenticeship at Chatham Royal Dockyards and had later become Manager of Fletcher & Fearnell. The partnership of Ditchburn & Mare first rented Dudman's Yard at Deptford, but a large fire in 1838 forced them to move and take over another site at Orchard Yard, Blackwall which had belonged to Gladstone Snook & Co., who had been in business there since 1823. They began with the construction of river steamers and progressed to cross-channel ships and then found themselves on the Admiralty list, but Ditchburn decided to retire from this modestly successful business in 1846. This was not a major blow as C. J. Mare did very nicely on his own becoming more eager to take on the liability of producing much larger ships from vessels under 1000 tons to the 'Himalaya' at 3438 tons, launched in 1853. Mare also purchased land on the Essex side of Bow Creek in the area called Hallsville (later known as Canning Town) with the yards on either side being joined by a ferry or floating bridge that could carry 200 workmen at a time. The slipways remained at Blackwall but other workshops and facilities were built across the creek. Mare's success was not to last however, as he got into financial difficulties due to contractual problems and other miscalculations, but there is strong evidence to suggest that his involvement with racehorses both as a breeder and a gambler constituted to his downfall.

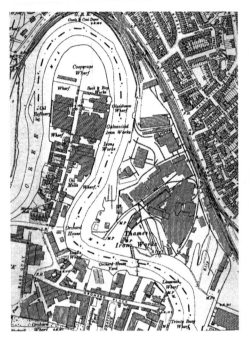

The Bow Creek area in 1895

Peter Rolt, Mare's father-in-law, then appeared on the scene. His credentials were impeccable. He was descended on his mother's side from Phineas Pett, Master Shipbuilder to James the First in the early 1600s. He was married to the daughter of the shipbuilder Gladstone Snook; he was director of the Commercial Dock Company, and a Conservative MP. In 1856 he became Chairman of the Board and assumed control, and the company was renamed Thames Ironworks & Shipbuilding Company.

As the company's difficulties were overcome the business developed and improved and in 1860 HMS Warrior was launched. At the time it was the biggest warship in the world and over its complete history to 1912 (including the ten years under C. J. Mare) Thames Ironworks built 146 warships besides numerous other vessels. Shipbuilding was not the only work carried out on the site, for with civil engineering projects such as bridge building and the supply of roofing, like that at Fenchurch Street station, electrical engineering, the manufacture of cranes, marine engines and later, motor cars, diversification was complete. Overall it was a phenomenal record of success.

A large part of that success in subsequent years came as a result of the energies and vision of one man – Arnold F. Hills. Born in 1857, he began his education at Harrow when he was 14 years old, going on to University College,

Arnold Hills

Oxford, where he also became a renowned athlete. In 1880, at the age of twenty-three he joined the board of Thames Ironworks, eventually becoming Managing Director. He not only devoted his life to the company, but to a certain extent, his workforce too.

Although the company had gone from strength to strength over the years, things did not always run smoothly at the yard as there was a dock strike in 1889 that spread to the Ironworks with boilermakers, labourers and joiners walking out. Even after settlement there were further strikes by joiners and engineers in 1890 and 1891 and during this awkward time Hills' relationship with his workmen was at an all-time low and 'scab' labour employed as replacements were badly treated by pickets on the gate. After this period of conflict Hills realised that changes needed to be made to labour relations and he introduced 'The Goodfellowship Scheme' which meant bonuses on top of standard wage rates. However, this did not prevent a disastrous strike in 1897/98 so Hills then tried a new approach by throwing out the Unions and negotiating with the men himself. He was one of the first to give his men a 48-hour week, which he combined with a profit-sharing scheme. Unfortunately this caused an increase in costs to the company that made it difficult to compete successfully with the northern shipyards for big contracts, as the northern concerns were closer to the raw materials of iron and coal. Another drawback was the location and lay-out of the yards, with 30 acres in West Ham and five in Blackwall, which restricted the company to any expansion, but Hills was not the type to abandon his men and their families by moving to a larger site such as those at Tilbury and Dagenham which were available at that time. He also raised questions about the lack of Government orders that the yard was receiving, but in 1910 the Navy gave him a contract to build the 'Thunderer', which at 22,500 tons was currently the Navy's largest dreadnought. It was launched in February 1911 but it turned out to be Thames' last big order, as it broke the yard financially. So a combination of negative factors led to Thames Ironworks, which had been a major source of employment in the area, sadly to decline and collapse in 1912.

Despite this decline in later years, Hills had already proved himself to be a model employer, for he improved the welfare, conditions and wages of his men. In his early years at the company, he lived out of choice in Victoria Dock Road for a period of five years, arranging his evenings to promote and organise the leisure and recreational facilities that he felt would be of great benefit to his workforce. He was responsible for the formation of many clubs and societies within the Works, with the football club being a latecomer in 1895. He was a keen vegetarian and took every opportunity to express his disgust about the evils of alcohol, being a main speaker at Temperance Societies, and sometimes going to bizarre lengths to prevent its consumption or use in any event.

Outside the work arena he had an interest in encouraging young people in self-help schemes, and his generosity led him to fund an Institute in Tottenham Court Road, London, which he named the 'Ideal Club'. The object of the club was to 'afford social enjoyment and recreation and educational advancement to young men and women engaged in business pursuits in London, especially those who were strangers to the capital'.

With so many business and leisure activities it was a wonder that Hills had any family life at all. However, he married Mary Elizabeth Lafone in 1886 and she bore him one son and four daughters.

In his later years it was both sad and ironic that such an individual, fit and healthy as a young man, and one who was forever interested in outdoor energies and pursuits, should fall victim to a wasting disease which left him almost totally paralysed. Such was his determination, however, that when the company went under in 1912 a campaign was launched to save it and on the 1st January of that year there was a large meeting in Trafalgar Square. Arnold Hills was there, prone on a stretcher, his frail, bearded face showing above the blankets. His men lifted him on to the plinth of Nelson's Column from where he addressed the meeting. Sadly it was all to come to nothing, and finally on December 21st 1912 a notice of closure was put on the main gate. Later another appeared signed by A. F. Hills. It read: *'Do not let such a notice spoil your Christmas. The fight is not finished and no battle is lost until it is won. I will not desert you in the darkest hour before dawn. I bid you be of good cheer.'*

Unfortunately the fight was indeed over and the property was sold off in 1914. The timing of the closure was ironic as the First World War began that same year when the need for extra shipbuilding was essential to counter the threat of the German High Seas Fleet. Thames' future would have been secured, but instead the enormous expertise within the company was wasted. Hills lived throughout the war years, and on to see the football club that he founded take part in the first Wembley F.A. Cup Final in 1923. He passed away in the house known as 'Hammerfield' in Penshurst, Kent on 7th March 1927.

Thames Ironworks' main office building and docks, facing the River Thames

CHAPTER ONE
ORIGINS
Pre 1895

During the early to mid 1890s, there were already a large number of football clubs, mostly amateur, but some professional, in existence in and around the Canning Town and West Ham district of the East End of London. The most notable ranged from the successful Clapton club, the re-formed Upton Park, Park Grove, West Ham Garfield and Claremont Athletic to the north of the district, to St Luke's, South West Ham, Old St Luke's and Castle Swifts in the south. To the west of the area were the Commercial Athletic and Millwall Athletic clubs, with the latter playing their home games at East Ferry Road, Isle of Dogs and turning professional in 1893. When the Southern League was formed in 1894/95 Millwall won the title in the competition's initial season. Further to the east were Barking Woodville, Barking and the Leyton club, which was to briefly embrace professionalism later in the decade, and Ilford who spent two seasons in the Southern League. At the end of 1895/96 Ilford quit the competition and lowered its sights after failing to gain a solitary point from 18 matches.

Many other clubs with varying abilities came and went over this period and one such club that had a briefer life than most was Castle Swifts, a club that can be said to have had a considerable influence on the formation of Thames Ironworks FC.

On the banks of the River Lea opposite the Thames Ironworks & Shipbuilding Company lay the ship repair yards of the Castle Shipping Line under the trading name of Donald Currie & Co. Employees at those yards were mainly Scots who came south to work for the shipping magnate Sir Donald Currie, who was responsible for the creation of the Castle Shipping Line in 1862, later in 1900 to be merged with the rival Union Line and become the famous Union Castle Line.

In September 1892 the Castle Swifts FC was born with most of the team initially being drawn from members of the Scottish workforce at Donald Currie & Co. The club's first home ground was at the field opposite West Ham Police station in West Ham Lane. The ground was enclosed, with a charge of 3d for admission and it was named 'Dunottar Park' after the Company's steamship 'Dunottar Castle' built in 1890, a ship that sailed on her maiden voyage from Southampton with the British rugby team on board for a tour of South Africa. Donald Currie himself presented the South African Rugby Authority with a handsome gold cup for internal competition and the Currie Cup has remained the holy grail of South African rugby right to this day. Amongst other voyages the Dunottar Castle was to carry General Buller and 1500 British troops to the Boer War in South Africa in 1900.

Castle Swifts FC did not have long to enjoy its first home however. Through a dispute with the landlord the club were obliged to quit, but a new ground was soon found not far from East Ham railway station, in fields flanking Wakefield Street, known as Temple Meadows in the grounds of Temple House. This was conveniently situated for changing purposes at the nearby Denmark Inn (now the Denmark Arms, and a watering hole for a pre-match drink for 21st Century West Ham fans).

Local leagues had not quite got off the ground at this time and the fixtures of the Castle Swifts were made up of cup-ties and friendly matches, although the latter were very much fought out in a competitive manner. The club also ran a youth side calling themselves Castle Swifts Juveniles and they had many victories against local minor teams.

Throughout this last decade of the 19th Century, despite our preconceived notions of Victorian efficiency, players and officials had to suffer inconsistencies in the rail transport system. Combined with this was the fact that most amateurs were obliged to work on a Saturday morning which meant a struggle to meet certain connections with horse drawn buses and steam trains. Referees, certainly at amateur level, appear to have been given a fair degree of flexibility and left to their own judgement regarding any amendment to kick off times or for bringing the game to a conclusion. It was not unknown for a match to be turned round at half-time and the whole ninety minutes played off in one period. On occasions whole teams might arrive late and at other times individual players could miss the start of a match. It must be remembered that there were no substitutes to fall back on, perhaps just a twelfth man taken only as a last resort.

An example of this type of situation came in Castle Swifts first season when they met St Luke's in a London Junior Cup tie in November 1892. The kick-off was originally scheduled for ten minutes to three, which for a murky, late autumn day was not exactly early anyway. Even so, one player on each side failed to arrive for the start. When they did make an appearance, at different times, the referee must have decided that such interruptions were time consuming for he did not blow his whistle for half-time until nineteen minutes to four, i. e. six minutes for wasted time! Due to this decision he allowed an interval of four minutes only, so the second half began at a quarter to four, but because the light was fading badly the referee blew for time at 4.21, nine minutes short. The game was not considered abandoned and was not replayed. This was far from an isolated case, but matches cut short by fog appear to have been treated more stringently.

Castle Swifts enjoyed good support from its company employees, and at the above match the local press reported somewhat amusingly that *a number of the fair sex were present, 'maistly Scotch' to judge from their enthusiastic shouts. 'Eh, the canny laddies' and 'stick to the ba Mac.'*

Although the club lost the above match it had quite a splendid first season. It was understood to be a professional concern from the outset, but this was not strictly true as it was more likely to have been a semi-professional or sham amateur outfit with the majority of their players being Scottish employees of Donald Currie & Co., paid on a game-to-game basis. Even in the club's first campaign amateurs were engaged such as the McFarlane brothers (A. & W.) who were members of the Upton Park club re-formed in 1891. This mix of Company team spirit and first class experience from outside helped to pave way for a path to the final of the West Ham Charity Cup (played at the Spotted Dog ground) in which the club emerged victorious after beating Barking Woodville by 4-2, after being two goals down. For the record, the Castle Swifts line up was:- Lewis, A. McFarlane, Benbow, Leith, W. McFarlane, Baird, Murray, Mitchell, Fraser, Taylor, Grundy (Scorers Grundy, Mitchell, Taylor and one own goal).

The local press reported that *'After the match the crowd made a rush to the Grand Stand where the Mayor presented the large silver cup to the captain of the Castle Swifts and Mr Comerford of the Cup Committee announced that 'the medals had not yet come to hand, but they would be forwarded to the winners as soon as possible'. With that the captain was lifted on to the shoulders of several of his followers and carried from the ground.'*

The following season of 1893/94 saw a further number of individuals that were certainly not professionals making appearances in the Castle Swifts team; they included Walter Parks, John Wood and William Hickman, who were officially members of the Old St Luke's club and future players of Thames Ironworks FC. Whether their inclusion in the side was due to injuries or through lack of choice of good players within the works of Donald Currie & Co. is not known, but at the end of the season Castle Swifts amalgamated with Old St Luke's and played their home games on the latter club's ground at Hermit Road, Canning Town. This venue would also have the benefit of convenience as it became increasingly obvious that their current home at Temple Meadows, East Ham was too far from their work's base on the banks of the River Lea.

It is of interest to note that at the time of the amalgamation, Old St Luke's honorary secretary was Mr A. C. Davis, who was later to become a Director of West Ham United in two spells from 1900 to 1906 and 1923 to 1949.

The amalgamation of the two outfits saw the new club competing, unsurprisingly, under the name of Old Castle Swifts in 1894/95, and although there was no silverware to add to that which was won two seasons before, the vast majority of matches ended in victory, including a splendid 4-0 conquest of Woolwich Arsenal reserves in January 1895. Naturally, there were a number of ex-Old St Luke's players in the side at various times such as Furnell, Butterworth, Sage, Morrison, Wood, Parks and Stewart. All would later appear for Thames Ironworks FC with most of them already in employment at the shipyard. In addition, Old Castle Swifts obtained ex-Millwall players such as Willing, Cunningham, Jamie Lindsay and Frank McCulloch, with the last two named eventually appearing for the 'Irons'. Even Bob Stevenson, Thames' future captain, although still on Arsenal's books, turned out for Old Castle Swifts in March 1895, just a few weeks before the club collapsed and disappeared from the footballing scene altogether.

It is not known why the club's demise came so suddenly. Perhaps their initial decision to pay their players turned out to be an unnecessary expense. Considering their gradual acceptance of local amateur players into the team this could well have been the case. Maybe there was not the drive and ambition to push the club on that there was to be at Thames Ironworks, or maybe it was not considered to be important enough to consistently spend extra money upon. After all, were it not for the financial backing of Mr Arnold Hills, in the five year existence of Thames Ironworks FC and his involvement in the early years of West Ham United, football in the East End of London may have followed a very different path.

It is worth recording that after Old Castle Swifts 'went under' at the end of March 1895, a pre-arranged fixture with St Luke's was fulfilled by their ex-players on 16th April, and for this one match only they went under the original name of Old St Luke's. The side included Furnell, Butterworth, Cooper, Morton, Parks and Wood, all keen players eager to get a game whatever the name of the club!

'Champing at the bit' after the demise of Old Castle Swifts was the St Luke's club whose ground was situated off the old Beckton Road. (There never had been any connections with the defunct Old St Luke's). At their AGM on 4th September 1895, the Secretary's report proved the club to be in a sound condition. Mr Anderson, Chairman of the club, stated that '...now the Old Castle Swifts are no longer in opposition there is room to make the club one of the best in the south of England. We have a good team, and the committee expects that every member of it will do his utmost to further the interests of the club.' Dave Furnell, who had now joined the team after the fall of the Old Castle Swifts, was elected as captain, with Butterworth also ex-Old Castle Swifts, as vice-captain. Decisions were made to compete for the London Senior Cup, Essex Senior Cup and the West Ham Charity Cup and also participation in the first season of the South Essex League.

The Beckton-based club did not realise at this time what impact the introduction of a works team from the local shipbuilding yards would have on the future of football in the area, ignoring the fact that a number of experienced players employed at Thames Ironworks had already 'kicked the leather' for a number of local sides including Old St Luke's, Castle Swifts, South West Ham, Plaistow Melville and Park Grove.

In that 1895/96 season, the 'Saints' did, however, enjoy a good campaign. The South Essex League came into existence and the club finished runners-up to Leyton, beating the eventual champions 4-1 in their home fixture. In fact, any other season would have seen them finish top, as they won nine and drew one of their twelve matches with a goal difference of 40 for and 15 against.

It was something of a surprise therefore, that the following season saw the club collapse. They were defeated by Ilford in the F.A. Cup at the end of October 1896 and withdrew from the South Essex League in the following January, after fulfilling less than a handful of fixtures.

All local clubs at this time, whether their existence was short or not seemed to have a hard core of support, but like today, there was always the irresponsible element. After St Luke's cup-tie defeat, the referee Mr Kirkup, was proceeding along Beckton Road towards the Abbey Arms when he received a severe blow from a stone thrown by a youth, who was later apprehended and, it was said, 'taken to the lock-up'.

Another club in close proximity to the Ironworks was South West Ham. Like parish side St Luke's, they had been formed in the 1880s and were the first in the district to give local working-men an opportunity to take part in 'the athletic and healthy pursuit of football and experience a competitive winter sport.' The team provided some excellent players over the years, including Billy Barnes, who also appeared for Thames Ironworks in 1895/96, Sheffield United and West Ham United, and went on to have along professional career, and Aubrey Fair who captained Russell Road schoolboys as a fourteen year old and later spent six seasons with West Ham United from 1901.

South West Ham's splendid enclosure and headquarters were close by Tidal Basin Railway station and the ground was used for cricket in the summer months as it had been since 1874 when the cricket club was formed. With easy ground access and the nearby facility of a frequent train service to the City, the club were in a good position to promote themselves further, but they were not particularly ambitious, being content to exist as an amateur outfit and serve the local community. The football club continued into the early years of the 20th Century, but the cricket club were a successful side, enjoying their best period in the 1920s when they included players of County standard, one being bowler Jimmy Harrold, who also played as an amateur footballer for West Ham United, albeit in the reserve side. When Silvertown Way was built in the early 1930s the whole ground was swept away, and the club had to move to a pitch at the rear of West Ham Stadium, but the club became defunct at the start of World War II.*

As far as football was concerned Thames formed a close relationship with the 'Pink Uns' as the South West Ham club was known, and several of the Ironwork's employees had periods of playing for both clubs at various times.

So the period surrounding the birth of Thames Ironworks FC was a time of constant change. The St Luke's club (the 'Saints') established for around ten years, collapsed in January 1897. Old St Luke's (the 'Old Uns') also around since the 1880s, were amalgamated with Castle Swifts, a club formed in 1892 with high hopes and business backing, but after becoming Old Castle Swifts were dead and buried by 1895. South West Ham (the 'Pink Uns') and Thames Ironworks (the 'Irons') both existed side by side throughout the last five years of the nineteenth century, but both were

* South West Ham played in the South Essex League (from 1895/96) and later the Eastern Suburban League (1899/1900). It has been suggested that the club were previously known as the Victoria Swifts but this is incorrect. The latter, although playing in the same area of Victoria Docks, played in the London Minor League over the same period of time. South West Ham took them over in 1900. Charlie Paynter, a future manager of West Ham United, originally played for Victoria Swifts and South West Ham before signing for West Ham United, where he played in the reserve team until joining the training staff.

heading in different directions. All those clubs can be said to have definite links and some bearing on the birth and formative years of Thames Ironworks FC, but it would not have been possible without a considerable number of working men, who after a hard week's toil, were eager play the game for some or all of the teams at one time or another over those years. Almost forgotten in the mists of time, these small, modest, unpretentious clubs should be recognised as the foundations upon which Thames Ironworks FC and its successor, West Ham United grew to become larger and more ambitious.

The popularity of the game in the 1890s also saw the advent of minor football. That is to say another level existed outside that of schools' football. Some clubs ran junior sides such as the Castle Swifts Juveniles and Thames Ironworks Juniors. We have already seen that Castle Swifts amalgamated with Old St Luke's, but in 1892/93 a minor side of 13 year-old boys was formed calling themselves Old St Luke's. Whether the team was a junior side of the original club is not known, but the lads stayed together as a team and after their first four seasons they had the incredible record of having played 114 matches with 104 wins, 3 draws and seven defeats with 558 goals for and 49 against! As the younger men matured the club provided five players for the 'Irons' including Fred Corbett and James Bigden, who both eventually went on to play for West Ham United and then continued their careers with other clubs.

It must also be acknowledged that there were two clubs in the wider area of the local district that had an earlier influence, albeit indirectly. Firstly Upton Park, one of the oldest clubs in the south, formed in 1866, just three years after the formation of the Football Association, who played their matches in West Ham Park. They were one of the fifteen original entries in the first-ever F.A. Cup competition of 1871/72 and participated for many seasons afterwards. Players of the 'Scarlet & Black' gained representative honours for both London and Essex and some made full international appearances such as Clem Mitchell who played for England on five occasions. Charles Alcock, recognised as the founding father of the Football Association and organiser of the modern game, was a member of the club from 1869 to 1872. Upton Park, unwittingly, played a part in the recognition of professionalism in the game in 1884, when after an F.A. Cup tie at Preston, they appealed to the F.A. that the home side had fielded paid players and Preston were subsequently disqualified from the competition. There had already been rumours of payments to players of northern clubs so the F.A.'s decision was significant as the problem was brought to a head. The following year, after a vote, professionalism was accepted and the whole structure of the game was altered for ever.

Most of the members of the Upton Park club were drawn from the nearby area of Forest Gate, a district full of large houses and upper class residents, and the majority of the players in the side were ex-public schoolboys; their occupations ranged from surgeons to solicitors, stockbrokers, surveyors, barristers, clergymen, accountants, tea merchants and many more of that ilk. This was a club of pure amateur players, built on the idea of 'muscular Christianity', where professionalism was taboo, and only the elite of society would be accepted. The idea that a riveter, a boilermaker or a plate-layer from the local shipbuilding yards would take his place in the side would not be considered at this time.

To their credit, ex-University and public school men did spread the gospel of the game far and wide from the 1870s onwards, unaware perhaps of the social impact that the sport would have, especially in the north of England, where the administrators there quickly turned it into a 'business first, sport second', with local working men finding a financial reward for their athletic endeavours. Unfortunately, with the administrators seeking instant success the locals in these clubs would soon find themselves forced out by the pure professionals recruited from Scotland and other parts of the kingdom. Meanwhile the pure amateur at Upton Park, with the only reward that of being able to play the game, would continue to appear for his local side or any club close by that was 'untainted' with professionalism. Gradually however, the influence of the Old Boy teams from the universities would decline, as did the Upton Park club, which was wound up in 1887.

Although the club rose again in 1891, with its acceptance procedure not so strictly enforced and including such local working lads as Ernie and Fred Roberts, Upton Park FC never regained the reputation that it previously enjoyed. There is an interesting post-script to their 'second coming'; the club was chosen to represent Great Britain in the 1900 Olympic tournament in Paris and won the competition beating France in the final without celebration and very little post-match publicity!

Arnold Hills, Chairman and Managing Director of Thames Ironworks & Shipbuilding Co. was an ex-public schoolboy and university man himself, and was instrumental in the foundation and establishment of his company's football club. He had also enjoyed a successful footballing career in his earlier days, playing for Oxford University in the F.A. Cup Final of 1877 and gaining a runners-up medal. Two years later he was capped for England against Scotland. His sporting prowess also extended to athletics as he was the A.A.A. one-mile champion whilst at Oxford.

There were no firm links between Thames and the Upton Park club, although solicitor Harold Lafone, a brother-in-law of Arnold Hills, was a member of Upton Park FC from 1881 to 1886, and played at outside-left in the first ever London Senior Cup final when the club beat Old Foresters 4-0 in 1883.

The other successful and reputable club in the district was Clapton FC. They conveniently came into the limelight in 1888 after Upton Park disappeared from the scene one year earlier. As London Junior Cup holders they moved to the Spotted Dog ground in Upton Lane at that time, a venue that had been previously used by St Bartholomews Hospital. In the following season they won the London Senior Cup, beating Royal Arsenal on the way to the final, and the Middlesex Senior Cup. 1890 saw them lift the West Ham Charity Cup followed by the Essex Senior Cup in 1891. The club was therefore well established with a number of trophies in the cabinet by the time the 'Irons' came on the scene.

Considering that Clapton was purely amateur, the club's committee was not lacking in enterprise, often arranging a number of fixtures against Football League opposition and competing in several cup competitions including the F.A. Cup. They were founder members of the Metropolitan Amateur League, and also the Southern League, which originated in 1894. Entry into the latter however, proved to be a mistake as most of the opposing clubs were already professional outfits, with the remainder soon to follow. With a poor playing record after two seasons, and realising that trying to compete on a regular basis with professionals was not to their advantage, they withdrew. On the plus side a number of the team members gained representative honours with London F.A.

Most of Clapton's players came from a middle to upper class background, but the ability, quality and skill of the men in the side overrode any matters of class distinction between the club and its supporters, who were mainly the workers of the Great Eastern Railway employed at the nearby Stratford Works, where there was a large enough base to maintain healthy support of the club providing it continued to produce the entertainment for which it was renowned, which it did over the last decade of the 19th Century despite the ever encroaching advance of the professional clubs which would however, eventually lure support away to the developing West Ham United and the more-established Tottenham Hotspur.

During its peak period the Clapton club, affectionately known as the 'doggies', had a regular following of 4,000 spectators. The amazing thing is that they all entered through a small gate, one by one. There was no shelter, and the field was initially just roped off, until iron rails later replaced the ropes. Originally players used a barn as a dressing room until the 'Spotted Dog' pub was used for a period of time. The first improvements came when wooden crate sides were laid down for standing, and a small member's stand erected where accommodation was provided for four members of the Press. After well over one hundred years, the Spotted Dog ground is one of the oldest remaining, despite some very close calls to develop it.

Over this great decade of change, with the blossoming of some clubs and the demise of others, and the growth in the number of players and the increase in spectators from 1890 to the dawn of the 20th Century, the local district has been rightly described as a hotbed of football. In the early part of the 1890s however, the football editor of the 'West Ham Herald' was not satisfied with the progress of the game in London and stated his case for the future in his football editorial in January 1892 after a week-end of F.A. Cup matches:-

'I wonder what the London players think of themselves. Not a single team can get through the first round, and yet you hear on some sides of London very soon becoming the centre of Association football. It will have to vastly improve before such an event occurs. The reverses the Southern teams have met with should be the means of causing them to look to their laurels, and to give such attention to football as would place them on a footing, at any rate, with the Northern and Midland clubs. How long the players of the South will allow themselves to be eclipsed by their Northern confreres is a question that requires immediate attention. There has been plenty of talk about starting a first-class team for London, but hitherto matters have ended in talk only. Surely, there is now sufficient enthusiasm in the game to support a good team in London, and it is my firm conviction that in no part of London would such a team take better than in Forest Gate—easy of access and full of football enthusiasts. We have, it is true, some fair teams in the neighbourhood, and as football goes in the South, Forest Gate is more fortunate than most places, and the clubs get well patronized. But only fancy what support a club would get which could announce fixtures with the League clubs and hold its own against them.'

The writer of the above must have had an insight into the future or a crystal ball as there certainly would be a club in the vicinity of Forest Gate within a dozen years of his above article at the nearby Boleyn ground at Upton Park, although it would not be until 1919 that the West Ham United club would be competing with Football League sides after a number of seasons in the Southern League.

The argument, however, of there being no first-class team in London at that time (1892) would soon be proved a fallacy as Woolwich Arsenal entered the Football League Division Two in 1893, Fulham in 1907 and Tottenham Hotspur in 1908. All those clubs had progressed from humble beginnings but as for the Chelsea club, it did not exist until 1905 when Mr H. A. Mears, a rich man by the standards of the day and who owned Stamford Bridge decided to develop it as a football venue and 'manufacture' a new club by persuading star players from other clubs to join the new venture. Forgive the author's cynicism, but it seems a bit familiar somehow!

Footnote: In other local histories and those of West Ham United it is stated that Old Castle Swifts amalgamated with St Luke's. This is not correct. Old St Luke's and St Luke's were two distinct clubs that had existed since the 1880s and often met in opposition. As explained in this chapter, the Castle Swifts club was formed in 1892 and amalgamated with Old St Luke's for the 1893/94 season, becoming Old Castle Swifts. After two seasons the club collapsed. It was not until halfway through Thames Ironworks' second season in January 1897 that St Luke's also disbanded.

CHAPTER TWO
FOUNDATION
1895/96

Although Dave Taylor, a foreman in the shipbuilding department, undertook the task of forming a football club within Thames Ironworks in the summer of 1895, the idea was not his alone nor was it a 'spur of the moment' decision. With the demise of the Old Castle Swifts there were a number of its former players who were employed at the Ironworks and now found themselves without a club. Players like Johnny Stewart, George Sage, Walter Parks and Jamie Lindsay amongst others, who would make the nucleus of a useful side. Their proposal backed by Dave Taylor, who was a local referee in his spare time, was to approach Arnold Hills, the Managing Director, and obtain approval of the idea of a football club within the Works, and give it his blessing. His approval came, and with it, over the five years of its existence, a great deal of financial help.

There were already a large number of societies and clubs within the Company. With cycling, athletics and cricket clubs for the sporting types, the military band, operatic society, orchestral band and choral society for the artistic, and the temperance league, ambulance corps and literary & debating society for the more serious, it was surprising that there had never been one covering football, although in 1892/93 a junior football team had been formed called Thames Ironworks Minors, but it had not been part of the Social club itself. In three seasons they had an astonishing 75 victories from 81 matches played. They continued to play during the

The Marquis of Salisbury in 2005

1890s as Thames Ironworks Juniors, competing in the Walthamstow League with varying success.

To Dave Taylor fell the initial organisation and administration of the new club, leading up to its first season. Membership cost two shillings and sixpence for the season, which was a large sum at that time, especially more so for those who were not likely to gain entry into either the first team or reserves. It was at first thought that four teams could be run but that did not prove practical, and it would have been too expensive.

Permission was obtained to use the ground vacated by the defunct Old Castle Swifts at Hermit Road, Canning Town. The ground was surrounded by a moat, with canvas sheeting used for fencing erected to 'hide play from non-paying spectators'. As they had been for the Old Castle Swifts, the dressing rooms were initially situated at the Marquis of Salisbury pub at the junction of Blanche Street and Hermit Road, just two minutes from the ground.

Dave Taylor had the unenviable job of arranging fixtures, as the club had not entered a league, but he gained affiliation to the F.A. and rather optimistically entered for the F.A. Cup. Before the season began however, he resigned his post to carry out his local refereeing duties and Mr A. T. Harsent took over as secretary of the club, and at the request of the players, a committee was formed of non-playing members of staff, being comprised of foremen and clerks.

Their opening game saw them take on the reserve side of the Woolwich club, Royal Ordnance, at Hermit Road, Canning Town on 7th September 1895. From the 'Kentish Mercury' it was reported that *'the home team won the toss and elected to play with the sun and wind at their backs. Despite this advantage, however, it was not until about 30 minutes from the start when their outside-left Darby, received the ball upon the 12 yard line and promptly sent it past Henshall who had no chance whatsoever of saving the shot. The visitors equalised in the 70th minute following a scramble in the Ironwork's goalmouth'.*

The following three Saturdays saw three consecutive victories before the trip to Chatham in the F.A. Cup. After the Ironworks were initially drawn at home, Chatham suggested that the Hermit Road enclosure, with its cinder-based pitch, was 'unsuitable' and requested that the tie be played on their ground. The Ironwork's committee may have been swayed by the prospect of a much bigger gate and extra revenue and they agreed to the change. After all, they had no real support at this early stage.

As it turned out, the attendance of 3,000 justified their decision from a financial viewpoint but it was no surprise that Chatham went through to the next round. They were a club of long-standing who had first entered the F.A. Cup in 1882/83 and had a creditable record in the competition. In 1888/89 they fell at the Quarter Final stage after battling through four qualifying rounds and three rounds proper.

As for the match itself, the visitors played fairly well in the middle of the park, but they were generally lost when near to goal. With Chatham 2-0 up at half-time, the home side wore the inexperienced Ironworkers down in the second half. Watson, in goal, misjudged the ball for the third goal, although he played well overall, whilst the rest of the defence had a torrid time keeping the score down. The only forward who did well for Thames was their most experienced player, Jamie Lindsay.

Undaunted and a little wiser, the club continued their schedule and two weeks later took on the reserve team of Reading, whose first eleven were competing in the Southern League. Thames put on a reasonable performance, despite being beaten by the odd goal in five.

Following four consecutive victories however, confidence began to grow and the club travelled to take on the first team of Dartford from the Kent League, who after having been forced to scratch a previously arranged fixture, agreed to play the Ironworks. The local reporter from the 'Dartford Express' was not best pleased at the idea and expressed his forthright opinions as follows:- *'Being unable to get a better team, the Committee arranged a match with Thames Ironworks and in so doing caused universal disappointment, for although the Thames men were known to have done some good things and to be a fairly stiff lot they were looked upon as being vastly inferior to the locals, and of such a calibre as to make a match with them lowering to the dignity of Dartford.'*

Not content with that he continued *'The match and all that attended upon it was significant of many things, the one most prominent being that it will not pay the Dartford committee to arrange matches with teams like the Ironworks. The result of such encounters, proving that the Dartford men play as they ought to, is always a foregone conclusion, and in view of this they are absolutely devoid of interest.'*

His little outburst would come back to haunt him when Thames next came to Dartford for an F.A. Cup match four years later, as will be seen. As for the game – it started late, there was a snowstorm at half-time, and it ended in the dark, so maybe the local reporter had really had enough and he showed it!

A 0-2 defeat was no disgrace for the Thames' men, and it was interesting to note that A. Williams, Dartford's captain in the previous campaign of 1894/95, was a member of the Ironwork's team. He was loudly cheered by the locals when he appeared on the pitch, and he gave quite a prominent display, making several shots on goal during the game. He continued to be a valued member of the team throughout their first campaign, but returned to Dartford during the 1896/97 season.

Let us not forget Dave Taylor, now concentrating on his first love – refereeing. He was the official in the middle when Thames Ironworks reserves played a friendly against a Barking Junior side by the name of Loxley FC, in November 1895. Dave reported J. Smith, the captain of Loxley to the Essex F.A, for the use of foul language and for inciting members of his team to misconduct. It was agreed that the player would be suspended until the end of the calendar year, but it is amusing to record that when cautioned Smith said that he didn't care if he was suspended, as he could then play for a rugby club!

The week after the Dartford match the Irons were entertained by Millwall reserves at East Ferry Road where a 0-6 drubbing was handed out, a result that turned out to be the biggest defeat of the season. The 'Thames Ironworks Gazette' tried to pull the wool over their readers' eyes when it stated that *we could not get a full representative team for the Millwall fixture, and had to put men in the team who hadn't kicked a ball for three years.'* In actual fact, the side, with one exception, was the same that had played the previous week!

On the following Monday came the great experiment – football by electric light. This was an event that was not unique as it had been previously tried on a number of occasions beginning as far back as 1878 at Bramall Lane Sheffield, and at other locations in the north of England and in Scotland that same winter. Without a common source of electricity at the time, any lights were provided by means of dynamo machines powered by batteries or steam engines. It was not a great success due to the varying strengths of the electrical systems employed, which could cause an uneven spread of lighting, strong shadows, and leave some areas of the pitch in the dark. In some cases the machinery used broke down altogether. Add on the vagaries of the weather, especially the wind that would rock those lights that were positioned on high poles, and rain that could interfere with the electrics, some mist or sudden fog, and it is not difficult to understand why it did not become permanent although there were further attempts during the 1880s and 1890s with varying success. It was regarded however as a novelty and with the advent of the Football League in 1888/89 it was important that fixtures were completed satisfactorily without unreliable electrical systems breaking down. Had the first experiments been carried out some years later when the whole country was covered by the National Grid system, with a uniform means of delivering and fine-tuning the system, then floodlit football may have come to Britain earlier than it did. Ironically, when this became available the Football League and the Football Association were too entrenched in their ideas to give it any serious consideration until the early 1950s when it began to receive official approval in this country.

Thames' original idea for using lights was, of course, financial. It was thought that if spectators could be attracted to the game under artificial light as well as the usual Saturday afternoon, then further matches could be arranged in midweek and that would add to the club's coffers. Provided that the initial experiment was at least moderately successful this would enable the Thames Ironworks' committee to go ahead and arrange a number of matches and improve the lighting as time went on.

The first match was fixed for Monday 16th December 1895 at Hermit Road, the opponents being Old St Stephen's from West London who were beaten 3-1. The overall 20,000 candle-power of light was driven by a large generator operated by men from the Ironworks, 'at great expense' according to the committee. Ten lights of 2,000 candle-power each were suspended on poles spaced at intervals around the pitch, making them somewhat dangerous to players and vulnerable to a misplaced pass or clearance. When the lamps failed together due to a malfunction of the generator, play had to be halted, but when the light returned it varied from bright to downright dim, so by all accounts the experiment was not a great success.

Not to be deterred the committee tried again in January, when Barking Woodville were the visitors. There were no great changes to the equipment although the causes of the generator breakdowns were resolved for according to various reports the occasion was a success. One local scribe began: 'The Thames Ironworks Social Club, whose motto ought to be 'Nil Desperandum' tried their luck again last night with success at Canning Town when they carried out the above match by electric light'.

Another report stated '...the occasion was a success. The engine (i.e. the generator used to power the lights) which was a gigantic one, met the requirements and was worked well under the supervision of one of the Company's servants. Ten lights each of 2,000 candle power gave a good view to those present.' For the record the Irons ran out easy winners by 6-2 with Charlie Dove scoring a hat-trick.

Both matches had attracted over 1000 spectators. Maybe favourable word got around and a greater number decided to see for themselves what this phenomenon was all about because a crowd of 3,000 witnessed the following game under the lights in February 1896 when Royal Ordnance provided the opposition. Although not entirely a success, due to the unexpected misty weather, not any fault of the equipment, the match was by no means a failure and the TIFC committee decided, in view of the interest taken to persevere with the exercise. In any case the gate receipts exceeded the cost of the operation and that was one important aspect of the whole undertaking.

The 2-1 result meant another victory for the Ironworks. Eleven days later the fourth match 'under the electric light' took place and an innovation was introduced when the ball was dipped in a bucket of whitewash to make it more visible. How many times during the game this disruption occurred or whether the players kit was covered in white blotches is not recorded, but the main point was that once again the attendance was high enough to cover the cost and make a profit.

A long and detailed report of the game against Vampires appeared in the 'West Ham Herald' and selected extracts here give a delightful insight into the club's early days and the journalist's several touches of humour.

'The idea of the Thames Ironworks Social Club Ltd to study those who are prevented through their daily avocation from attending afternoon matches by carrying out those by the aid of electric light on their ground at Canning Town has certainly taken root judging by the big crowd that paid at the gate last evening to witness the contest.

(So) for the fourth time this season the Thames Ironworks football team were engaged...in a match by electric light, and the Vampires are no doubt congratulating themselves on being the first club to lower the Thames colours (under lights). From the fast manner in which the game opened one almost imagined that the teams were fighting out a cup tie in broad daylight.

......Boys were swarming up over the fences for a free view when I put in an appearance. And what a smart man the Ironworkers have at the gate. He seemed to think my ticket was a real fraud until he had turned it upside down and inside out, and smelled at it for a considerable time. But he graciously passed me at last.

The Thames boys were first on the field, giving a preliminary exhibition of kicking while waiting for the arrival of the Vampires, and the crowd meanwhile *amusing themselves with jumping and stamping their feet as an accompaniment to the brass band. The Vampires turned up a bit late, and the game was not started till a quarter of an hour after the advertised time......Vampires started well, shooting at goal in the first five minutes. Then the Ironworkers got the ball and ran it down the field. The ball, by the way, was enamelled white and showed up well in the bluish haze of the electric light.*

The Vampires pressed very hard, and after twenty minutes play succeeded in notching the first goal, to the delight of their own supporters and to the dismay of TIW.

After a bit of a skirmish and plenty of give and take play, hands was given against the Thames but nothing came of it......A grand pass by Chapman was spoilt by what seemed like over-anxiety on the part of Captain Stevenson. Gresham played grandly, but seemed to be doing everything himself......The half was especially noticeable for the number of foul throws given against Vampires and the lamentable cry of one of the Vampire's supporters, who kept on calling out 'Vamp! Vamp!' and trying to be sarcastic to the boy with the necessary cough drops.

After the interval of ten minutes, referee Fundell brought the men up to scratch again......Thames were having all the play, though with no good result except penning the Vamps up in their own goal. But they got up and away however, and then Ward put the ball through the Ironwork's posts a second time. The referee disallowed a Thames claim for offside and the crowd howled in bloodcurdling style.

Thames seemed to lose heart over this second goal with the result that the Vamps scored another......then Thames put all they were worth into their play, and scored a goal. Party feeling among the spectators ran very high, and cheers were called for first by one side and then by the other. I have heard rumours of foul play by the Thames, but a more thoroughly gentlemanly game I never saw; in fact it was a fast, good game.

Football journalists reporting matches at the time have to be admired. Player's shirts were not numbered, nor would they be until the late 1930s, and identifying players in matches like the above game, especially for local reporters who were obliged to name those of the opposition, could not have been easy, and that would also apply in fog bound games and those finishing in twilight. Let us not forget their considerable contribution made to football history.

Three further matches were scheduled to be played under electric light during March 1896 and some improvements were made to the lighting equipment, so much so that criticism of this type of match was not so evident and the game against West Croydon was reported as if it were nothing unusual. Thames opponents however, seemed bemused by the conditions and were four goals down at the interval, with the Irons adding just one more in the second half after easing off the pedal.

The committee showed enterprise by arranging the final two fixtures against Football League clubs. When all is considered the Irons were only a works side and in their first season at that. To persuade such opposition to visit Hermit Road and play under unusual conditions must have been something of a coup. Once again a profit would be made, and perhaps more importantly the profile of the club would be raised considerably.

On Monday 16th March, Woolwich Arsenal, who were then in the Second Division of the Football League, fielded a strong side of mainly first team players. Graham, in the Thames goal had a busy night, but kept the score down as the interval came with the Irons 1-2 down. Play in the second half was chiefly confined to midfield during the first fifteen minutes as strong wind developed which had a detrimental effect on the game, but fortunately the electric lamps were not impaired in any way and the system thankfully did not break down. Gresham and Fitzjohn put

Thames back in the lead, but perhaps confirming the quality of the artificial light, Arsenal's Caldwell dribbled the ball expertly from one end of the field to the other and scored. At the end of the game the League side ran out winners by 5-3. The attendance was a profitable 2,000.

So to Thames final electric light encounter, which came on the following Friday evening. The opponents were Football League Division One side West Bromwich Albion, struggling to keep their status as they languished at the foot of the table. They had a pause in their League fixtures between March 9th and April 3rd and undertook a short tour of the South between those dates. They fielded a strong side, but to destroy a long-standing myth, Billy Bassett, the famous England outside-right, did not play, much to the crowd's disappointment. (The following day he was also absent from the Albion's line-up in a friendly at Wycombe).

This final evening encounter was not marred by inclement weather, so the League side, after the first fifteen minutes, adapted to the lighting conditions quite comfortably and ran out relatively easy winners by four goals to two, but although the Irons were unable to match the quality of the opposition they had the experience of playing a famous club from the top echelons of the game.

The Ironworks committee's initiative in undertaking the whole exercise of these matches by electric light had been fully justified. Despite the running costs, many workers had been able to see matches that they otherwise would not have done, a small profit had been made, and the profile of the club was made more conspicuous.

Aside from their engagements under artificial light the club still had a busy programme of friendly fixtures and West Ham Charity Cup games. The St Luke's club, not lacking in experience over the previous few years, were considered to be the Iron's closest rivals in the area, although when the two clubs met in February 1896 Thames had only been in existence six months, but such was their record (20 wins, 1 draw and only 7 defeats) the forthcoming clash was described as 'a contest to decide the championship of the district.' It was even suggested that should the Irons continue their winning ways they would probably find themselves in the Southern League the following season, but that was a premature prediction.

Just before kick-off saw the arrival of Mr & Mrs A. F. Hills who had driven over in their brake (a horse-drawn carriage) from their current home, 'Monkhams' in Woodford to witness the game. The local press considered this to be most praiseworthy and creditable stating that '...if this example were only followed by other large employers, it would lead to much good feeling.'

Both clubs fielded strong sides, although St Luke's had six players under treatment, three of whom had been obliged to remain off work during the week owing to injuries previously sustained. It is not known whether any of their employers took a sympathetic view of this or not. Stevenson, Thames' captain, headed a goal in the first half, and with the Saints striking the crossbar twice in the second half, the score remained at 1-0 to the home side, much to the delight of the majority of the crowd of 2000. Before the season's end the teams met twice more, with one game to St Luke's and one draw. Honours even!

Mr A. T. Harsent, the club's secretary, together with his committee members, could not be accused of lacking in inspiration. Despite financial assistance from Arnold Hills, they were always looking for new schemes to provide extra finance and to promote the club's image. This had been achieved by their entry into the F.A. Cup and the innovation of the matches by electric light. Now a further idea was proposed by arranging a fixture and combining it with the important launch of the battleship 'Fuji', a ship ordered by the Imperial Japanese Navy. This was one of many warships constructed at the Thames Ironworks & Shipbuilding Co. and a launch was always a special occasion. The 'Fuji' was a large battleship of 12,320 tons with a length of 412 ft and width of 73ft 9in. It had a life of just a few months under 50 years before it was destroyed in an air attack by the American Air Force in July 1945.

Taking advantage of the fact that there would be a large crowd at the launching ceremony, with the added bonus of a day's holiday already granted, the committee arranged a match against Royal Ordnance FC, the plan being that those people who had been to the launch would need somewhere to go to 'wind up' the holiday. The Thames Ironworks Military Band under their bandmaster Mr Hans, was always present at launching occasions, so it was decided that after the event the band should play and march to the Hermit Road ground, which would draw people along 'pied piper' fashion to the match, and so it proved. It must have been an impressive sight, with prospective spectators in tow, and street urchins striding and jumping to the music, but perhaps a little exhausting for the musicians marching along Hallsville Road and Rathbone Street, past Canning Town Hall and down Hermit Road to the ground whilst they tried to keep in step and simultaneously avoid the horse dung splattered on the cobbled streets along the way.

The match itself was keenly contested but the result was disappointing. The visitors had most of the play with Graham and his defence having a busy time. As it was Thames had enough open chances of their own but their shooting was woeful, and at the break the Ordnance boys were one goal up. After the interval the visitors scored again even though the Irons continued to attack, but they missed more chances with Stevenson being the main culprit. It was said on one occasion that 'he mistook the entrance gate for the goal.' Graham later saved a shot and then stepped back under the bar and conceded a goal. Following that Thames wilted and eventually Royal Ordnance finished winners by 4-0. It was a bit like 'after the Lord Mayor's Show'.

Just three weeks prior to this defeat Thames had been instructed to replay their semi-final tie in the West Ham Charity Cup against Park Grove. The original match had resulted in a victory for the Ironworks by 1-0, but Park Grove protested that Thames had fielded players who did not have the correct club and residential qualifications under the rules of the competition and this objection was upheld. The Ironworks' committee should have been well aware of this rule, since the reserve team took the field in the previous round of the West Ham Charity Cup competition in December 1895 against the reserve side of local rivals St Luke's, winning by five clear goals, whilst the first team was engaged in a friendly match at Dartford.

The replayed game took place at St Luke's ground at Beckton. The Ironworks had to play seven different men from the original match, and although it was mentioned in the local press that seven reserves had to play, this was not strictly the case as most of the so-called 'reserves' were very experienced players, who had in their time played more than their fair share of matches, not only for Thames but other local clubs as well. Their relative quality showed during the game as a thoroughly disorganized opposition were run off their feet. Thames' best two players were Johnny Stewart, who was 'strikingly prominent' and contributed much to the Irons success — and the captain, Stevenson, who scored two of the goals in a 3-0 victory. It meant they would meet Barking in the final at the Spotted Dog on March 21st 1896.

Thames made two changes from the side that beat Park Grove in the semi-final. Jamie Lindsay came in for Tull at right back and Billy Barnes took the place of Chamberlain in the forward line. Both replacements had been registered players with the Ironworks before the previous November's deadline and were ostensibly South West Ham players at this time, but as stringent as the qualification rules for this competition were it was not uncommon that 'guest' players were allowed to take part in the final.

The proceeds at the gate were devoted entirely to the funds of West Ham Hospital and with 3,000 spectators present the Charity committee were more than satisfied. It seems extraordinary that the Irons included four players in Graham, Sage, Stevenson and Chapman who had played just the evening before in that memorable meeting against Football League First Division opposition in West Bromwich Albion, but the committee would have wanted such players included in both games, and the players themselves would not have wanted to have missed either match.

The final itself was an exciting affair, with Barking's Inglis striking the cross-bar in the first minute or so. Play went from end to end with Woods and Williams tackling well in defence and soon the former put Stewart through for him to score after 15 minutes. Graham had to make a couple of fine saves before handball against Williams resulted in Inglis scoring for Barking just before half-time. In the second half Stevenson had a shot which hit the underside of the bar and McCappin, the Barking 'keeper, pulled the ball into his own goal. Barking did their utmost to equalise and it was not too long before Inglis did that scoring with a superb shot. Lindsay, easily the best back on the field, was injured and had to retire, which put the Irons under a lot of pressure, and Graham made an excellent save just before the whistle. So at 2-2 the final went to a replay, which took place a week later and finished as an uneventful scoreless draw. The second replay was fixed for three weeks later at St Luke's ground at Beckton.

The Saturday before the next replayed final, South West Ham visited the Hermit Road enclosure for the second time that season. Since the first encounter on Christmas morning the Hermit Road ground had undergone a transformation and Mr Harsent and his committee were congratulated upon their progress. Little did they realise at the time that the Ironworks would have to vacate their home just a few weeks after the start of the following season.

The local poet put pen to paper in anticipation of the match, with the title:-

PLAY UP IRON WORKS

Again another local team
    The Ironworks come to play,
And this game should be a good one
    That takes place here today,
For they have met here once before
    When the Ironworkers won the game,
And the 'Souths' have made their minds up
    That today shall not be the same.
So pluck up, old Ironsides,
    To win this match today
To beat these local rivals,
    And show how you can play
On Monday you meet Barking,
    And you'll win the Cup I think
So on Monday night Iron expects,
    Out of it to have a drink.

Graham, the goalkeeper that afternoon, was to be the only Thames player who would be in the Cup Final team on the Monday, but on the South West Ham side was Billy Barnes, who would also be assisting the Irons in the Cup final and become their match winning hero.

Three minutes from the start, Ridges succeeded in beating Graham and scored. After Shaw, of the Souths had had a good run, Hurst tackled and found Gresham who equalised. The 'Pinks' were demoralised for a while with the Ironworks doing all the pressing, and showing excellent combination play.

Souths then attacked and there was a sensational melee in front of the home goal, with Barnes being the prominent player, but shot after shot was repelled and Graham stood firm. Armit of the Souths then got clear on goal but was badly fouled, but nothing came of the free-kick. Then just on half-time Gresham scored to put the Irons ahead.

In the second half Dove and Gresham were always 'in evidence' for Thames whilst Collins worked like a demon at centre-half. Barnes netted for the 'Pinks' but the referee declared it offside. After a scrimmage in front of Chidley's goal, Oxspring (who was to play for the Irons two seasons later) whilst attempting to clear, put through his own goal to make the final result 3-1 in Thames' favour.

The choice made by the Cup Committee to use the ground of St Luke's at Beckton for the second replay of the West Ham Charity Cup final is an interesting one. The two drawn matches had both taken place at the Spotted Dog, the home of Clapton FC, and during the period of the early to mid 1890s the venue was considered to be the best appointed, most convenient and readily accessible ground for a number of local finals. However, Clapton's last home fixture of the season in the Southern League (and incidentally the club's last-ever in that league), fell on Saturday 18th April and it was arranged that the final of the West Ham Charity Cup would have to be played on the following Monday at 6.00pm. Having to play this second replay in midweek, a decision was made to use the St Luke's ground just off the Beckton Road as it would be the best option financially, and so it proved. With the venue situated within an easy distance of the Canning Town residents there were three thousand spectators pressed around the ropes when the players kicked off.

Wherever football matches were contested in West Ham in the area where those residents and workers lived such as the Hermit Road ground of Thames Ironworks, St Luke's at Beckton and the Tidal Basin ground of South West Ham, there was always the looming presence of the largest factory centre in the South East of England. Not only were the views of these industrial features hard on the eyes, the stench from the multifarious occupations that covered the district was an ever-present inconvenience, to put it mildly. The near proximity to the rivers Thames and Lea saw many industries rising along their banks. To the west of the Hermit Road ground lay the Poplar Gas Works, West Ham Sewage Works and Abbey Mills Chemicals, and of course the Thames Ironworks & Shipbuilding Company. Near to St Luke's ground at Beckton, Ceylon Mills which manufactured coconut matting, Paragon papermaking works and the Northern Outfall Sewer were situated, but the enclosure that suffered the most from obnoxious air was that of South West Ham FC at its Tidal Basin headquarters, as there were several riverside sites nearby containing a variety of manufacturing processes, mainly John Knight's soap factory, the rubber and gutta percha works of Silvers, the Tate Sugar Refinery, the company of Burt, Boulton & Haywood which distilled tar, creosote and disinfectant, and situated almost adjacent was Odams Chemical Manure Company which made manure from liquid blood provided from the company's slaughterhouse from cattle imported via Victoria Docks.

A vigorous breeze or change of wind direction and not just the immediate but the whole area suffered from this polluted air. After 90 minutes of football the players' mouths and throats would not only suffer but their lungs would be raw from the choking air into the bargain. However, this was the late Victorian age and it was all part of everyday life that differed greatly to that of today. These industries and many others were men's livelihood and the lifeblood of the district, and working men considered themselves fortunate to be employed at all.

It was against this background that both teams trotted out for the second replay of the Charity Cup Final, at the home of the St Luke's club, on a sunny, calm Monday evening in April, thankfully on this occasion devoid of any wafting fumes from the factories nearby. The attendance actually exceeded 3,000 on this occasion and the chairman of the Charity Cup committee, Mr W. Comerford, was beaming all over at the magnificent gate. He stated that although the whole funds for the season had yet to be calculated, with the total of the three final matches yet to be added, they were certain to be well up on previous years, with amounts in the past varying from £50 in 1888 to £115 in 1891, with lesser amounts in the years following due to Clapton and Ilford not competing.

As for the match Barking won the toss and decided, strangely enough, to play with the sun in their faces, without any benefit of a following wind. Whilst the whistle at an adjoining factory (almost certainly that of Ceylon Mills) was sounding six o'clock, Freeman kicked off.

It was all Irons right from the start with Freeman and Sage missing some good opportunities. Sadly for Barking, Langford, one of their forwards, had to retire from the field with an injury after 20 minutes and did not return. Woods, Barnes and Freeman all put shots behind. Barking then had a ten-minute spell but also lost their 'shooting boots'. It was 'nip and tuck' for quite a while afterwards with more chances being wasted by both sides but in one Ironwork's attack one of the Barking full-backs resorted to making a clearance with a vengeance, 'the ball being sent for a run somewhere along the Beckton Road.' It was end-to-end stuff with Barnes on one side and Inglis on the other going close, but the whistle went for half-time at an agreed period of 35 minutes, due to the six o'clock kick-off.

In the second half Stewart had a mazy run for Thames that was stopped by Emberson, then followed perhaps the most exciting period of the match as the Irons swarmed around the Barking goal, but could not score. One shot struck the crossbar and another one of the uprights and corner kicks came thick and fast, but Barking hit back on the break and Inglis scored with a great shot only to have it declared offside, but there was a doubt about the referee's decision.*

Graham then had to make two magnificent saves and Barking's positive play had to be admired as they had only ten men. Then ironically Thames lost Freeman to an injury so both sides were a man short. Sadly for Barking, they had the ball in the net again but this time it was clearly offside. Chamberlain then had a shot deflected for a corner, which Sage took and Barnes, with a low, fast shot, scored amidst loud cheering. Barking tried hard for the equaliser but full time arrived, with the Thames men triumphant. The full line-up of the first side to win a trophy in the history of the Thames Ironworks/West Ham United club was as follows:- Graham, Stevenson, French, Wood, Chapman, Hickman, Chamberlain, Sage, Freeman, Barnes, Stewart.

Just as Castle Swifts had won the West Ham Charity Cup in their first season, the Irons, three years later, now followed suit. It was an achievement that was all the more praiseworthy, considering that a number of first-team players were not available due to competition rules regarding club registration and residential qualifications. Chamberlain and Freeman were reserves, whilst Hickman and French were not exactly first choice at this late stage of the season. William Chapman was obliged to play at centre-half instead of in the forward line, due to Collins'

* Before the offside rule was altered in 1925 a player making a forward pass to a colleague had to have three opposing players between him and the goal-line at the moment he made the pass, so spare a thought for the referee and his linesmen in those days as it must have been something of a nightmare when it came to making the correct decision.

unavailability, and Billy Barnes, nominally a South West Ham player was drafted into the forward line. His inclusion however, proved to be a master stroke as the 16 year-old, just one month short of his 17th birthday, and due, eventually, to win an F.A. Cup winners medal and have a long and successful career, scored the only goal of the match.

To win a trophy is a cause for celebration, and celebrate is what the players did. It was not far from the St Luke's ground in Beckton to the Trinity School rooms in Barking Road and when the players had changed that is where they headed. Members of the Charity Cup committee were present together with officials of the Thames Ironworks FC. Mr Patterson (Thames) was elected to the chair and 'with genial tact ruled the realm of song and smoke'.

It must be noted that Mr Arnold Hills was absent from the evening's proceedings. It is possible that he had more urgent matters that claimed his attention or maybe he feared the probability that for most of the players a celebration would not be complete without the enjoyment of an alcoholic beverage or two. After all, his worthy club captain, Bob Stevenson 'passed round the flowing cup, the company drinking to the future prosperity of Thames Ironworks FC.' Not with barley water or lemonade, that's for certain.*

Notwithstanding any drink, the evening's entertainment was thoroughly enjoyable. By the standards of players of the 21st Century it might have been considered unexciting fare, but for these sturdy lads of the late nineteenth century it was the age of the 'song', a bottle of stout or two and a chance to let their hair down.

By their titles, the songs must have been mostly of a comic nature. Accompanied by Mr Patterson and the safe pair of hands of goalkeeper Graham on piano, there were such renderings as 'All the dogs went bow, wow, wow', from William Hickman, 'More work for the Undertaker' from George Edwards (South West Ham), Johnny Stewart's warbling of 'My gal ain't got eyes like diamonds', and old Tom Robinson, Thames trainer's rendition of 'Up went the price of meat'. Mr Arnold Hills might not have approved of Bob Stevenson's choice of song with his rendering of 'Drink boys, drink', and a particular ditty from reserve team player Mr Spruce would certainly give offence in today's world, entitled 'The Dandy coloured Coon'.

After a good time had been had by all, the club committee announced that they intended to hold an entertainment and dance at Canning Town Public Hall, when the medals would be presented and the Chairman, Mr Arnold Hills, would be in attendance.

This would be another occasion to look forward to, as apart from the player's weekly training and involvement in first or reserve team football there was very little of winter interest or entertainment to speak of compared to that of today. This was the reason why Arnold Hills formed his societies and clubs within the works, giving his employees the opportunity to take time away from the drudgery of their normal everyday lives. Outside the environment of the Company there was the local music hall, which is perhaps where some of the songs that were sung on the night of their celebration originated. If so, that would have been the Royal Albert Music Hall, originally known as Relfs (after its proprietor Charles Relf), a theatre situated at the northern end of Victoria Dock Road, later to become the Imperial Cinema. Of course,

---

Although Arnold Hills was anti-drink and a temperance leader there is no evidence that any strict embargo on players drinking alcohol existed, although the players would be unlikely to admit to any indulgences. As will be seen, it was not until Hills proposed the creation of the new club of West Ham United that he made teetotalism a condition, something that would soon prove to be overlooked anyway.

the pubs in the district were numerous and well frequented, much to the disillusionment of Arnold Hills and his anti-drink crusaders.

A number of football clubs had their headquarters in such establishments, one of those being the St Luke's club so it was to the 'Abbey Arms' pub that the defeated Barking team were invited after the final to receive their runners-up medals.

As a result of Thames' accomplishment in winning the West Ham Charity Cup, one of the largest attendances of the season gathered at the Hermit Road ground for the final match of this first campaign when Millwall reserves were the visitors. To show how much the club had progressed since the previous meeting between the same sides the final result was a 1-1 draw, compared to the 0-6 reverse in the first game back in December. Considering the Ironworks had seven of the same players appearing in both matches this confirmed their improvement. It is true of course, that Thames were opposing the reserves of Millwall, but they were a professional club and the Millwall first team, on this very day, were demolishing Swindon Town by 9-1 to take the Southern League title for the second successive season.

So ended Thames Ironworks FC's first season of 1895/96 and Mr Harsent and his committee must have felt a fine sense of achievement. They had built a club from scratch just a few months before, and by blending hard work and initiative together had won the majority of their fixtures and had also been rewarded with some silverware. To prove the club's strength in depth the second eleven also had a successful campaign winning 16 matches from a programme of 23.

However, a schedule of friendly games and the odd cup-tie or two were not enough to satisfy the ambitions of the committee or its players, so before the current season was over the club had already made application to join a league. In a meeting that had been held at Finsbury Barracks in March, Thames Ironworks FC were elected into the Second Division of the newly formed London League, but after Royal Ordnance decided to withdraw they found themselves taking their place in the First Division.

During Thames initial campaign, men from the Ironworks, who had originally been experienced amateurs with other local clubs, could expect to be involved in first team action or at least on the very fringe of it depending on form or injury. With the prospect of more important fixtures in the season to come, they would have to face the threat of extra competition for places from players brought in from outside.

In the close season, the Thames Ironworks Federated Clubs held an athletics meeting at the Hermit Road Ground. Besides the usual athletic and cycling events a foot race under handicap rules for members of the football club was arranged. The distance was one lap of the track, which was approximately 300yds. Captain Bob Stevenson obviously not known for speed was given 25yds start, French 18yds, Chamberlain 16yds (not exactly fleet of foot for a winger!), Patterson 15yds, Chapman and Charlie Dove both on 12yds, Farrell, Coxhead and Johnny Stewart all 10yds and John Woods at scratch. Bobby Stevenson kept the lead throughout but fell as he reached the winning post. However, he touched the tape without breaking it, and some of the spectators thought he should be disqualified, but the judges decided otherwise. French was second and Coxhead third, with the winning time being 44 seconds. Several of those players who contested the race would not be considered for inclusion in the first team for the following season of 1896/97.

Thames Ironworks in 1896, with the West Ham Charity Cup. Back; Arnold Hills (Chairman, Thames Ironworks), French, Graham, F Payne (secretary), Woods, Hickman and Robinson (trainer). Centre; Chamberlain, Sage, Stevenson, Chapman, Barnes. Front; Stewart, Freeman.

Pen Pictures

William Barnes *born May 20th 1879 died 1962*

It seems remarkable that Billy Barnes early football career, which began when he was just 16 years old with Thames Ironworks FC, has been  previously overlooked. He made at least five appearances for the club in its initial season of 1895/96 before joining South West Ham at Tidal Basin, where he appeared regularly for them in the South Essex League and in cup competitions. When Thames reached the final of the West Ham Charity Cup, the club was allowed to field a guest player providing he possessed the correct qualifying registration, and Billy, who had been with the Irons in the first half of the season fell into that category.

The final against Barking went to three matches and Barnes played in each one. Already, at this young age, a gifted left-sided player, he scored the only goal in the deciding game, so he should have been recognised as part of the club's folklore long before he came back to play for West Ham United in 1902/03 after scoring the winning goal in the previous season's F.A. Cup Final for Sheffield United.

After his early career at Thames Ironworks and South West Ham he signed on as a professional with Leyton in 1898, playing regularly for them in the South Essex League. After a string of outstanding performances he came to the notice of First Division League side Sheffield United the following year and played for them for three seasons. His first team outings were limited however, for he made just 23 appearances, scoring 6 goals in that period, but he gained a place in the replay of the 1902 F.A. Cup final and scored the winning goal in a 2-1 victory over Southampton which gave him a special place in the annals of Sheffield United where he was referred to as the 'Canning Town youngster.'

The following season a return south to his roots saw him with West Ham United where in two campaigns he made 48 appearances, scoring 5 goals. He signed for Luton in 1904 and was there for three seasons notching up 101 appearances with twelve goals. His longest spell at any one club came when he joined fellow Southern League club QPR. He remained there for six seasons scoring 37 times in 216 matches, gaining a Southern League Championship medal

in 1907/08. He was the club's top scorer in 1908/09, when the vast majority of his games were on the left wing. His last club, as a player was at Southend United in 1913/14 where he scored 4 goals in 17 matches. He made his final first team appearance in January 1914 and was finding it difficult to maintain the pace after such a long and effective career. So much so that the football critic of the Southend Telegraph stated that *'the affects of Anno Domini are showing'*. He played out the rest of the season in the reserve team and retired that summer. Not content with a career that covered 19 seasons he took up a coaching role with Athletico Bilbao in Spain after the First World War, and when West Ham United went on their first continental tour in 1921 the two clubs met with the Irons victorious by 2-1.

If we include Thames Ironworks and West Ham United records together Billy was the youngest player ever to appear in the first team. His first confirmed appearance came when he was just 16 years and 166 days old, but as a few early records are missing he may well have played for the club at an even earlier age.

William Chapman *born Canning Town, circa 1874*

Was with local parish side St Luke's in 1894/95, and began the following season with them, scoring a hat-trick in a South Essex League fixture against Forest Swifts before joining Thames Ironworks FC for their first campaign, in which William played in more games than any other player, notching up a confirmed 26 appearances, with 6 goals to his credit. In that first season many appearances and goalscorers sadly went unrecorded so it is certain that his actual figures were much higher. William was a front line player who could play in any forward position but he gained his West Ham Charity Cup winner's medal playing in defence in the final. Strangely, after such a consistent first campaign for the club he played in just two first team matches in 1896/97 and disappeared from the football scene altogether.

Arthur Darby *born Canning Town, Sept Qtr 1870*

Arthur began his career alongside Charlie Dove in the Plaistow Melville team in 1892/93. He turned out for Old St Luke's and then St Luke's in the following seasons, but his greatest claim to fame, as far as the history of the club is concerned, is that he was the scorer of Thames Ironwork's first ever goal in the opening day draw with Royal Ordnance reserves at Hermit Road on 7th September 1895. He also played in the club's first ever F.A. Cup match against Chatham. A number of appearance records from that first season are unknown, so there is no record of him having played in any further games in 1895/96, but he did play regularly for St Luke's for most of that period. After the St Luke's club disbanded halfway through the following season, Arthur played two matches for the Ironworks in the London Senior Cup, but did not play for them again. He was employed at the yard as an engineer's labourer.

(In July 1896 Thames Ironworks Federated Clubs held one of their athletic meetings at Hermit Road. One of the events was an extraordinary 'one lap football dribbling handicap' in which Arthur participated. He started at scratch, maybe because of his understood ability, but he finished in third place, whilst the eventual winner was given 10 yards start!)

Thomas Freeman *born Northfleet Kent, circa 1869*

As a small child, Thomas moved with his family to the East End and lived at Wouldham Street (now Road), West Ham. He played several matches for St Luke's in 1894/95 and appeared for them in the West Ham Charity Cup, the final of which was lost to Woodville (of Barking) by 2-4. He was employed as a Ships Fireman and played mainly in the Ironwork's reserve team. He did however, gain a cup winner's medal in the West Ham Charity Cup final of 1895/96, and he also appeared in the club's first ever F.A. Cup match against Chatham. As an adult he lived at 31 Hoy Street, just a 'stone's throw' from his previous address.

James Lindsay *born Scotland, circa 1870*

James, or Jamie, as he was more popularly known was essentially a forward, mainly leading the attack, but he did on several occasions put on some impressive performances at full back. He began with the Anchor club from East Ham, but his displays caught the eye of the Millwall club and he made a number of first team appearances for them in 1893/94 including a friendly match against Chesham which resulted in a 17-0 win and stands as Millwall's biggest ever victory of any sort. Jamie was credited with 4 goals in that match although the identity of scorers of only 11 of the goals was reported. The following season the East Ferry Road club entered the newly formed Southern League, and Lindsay found himself in the reserve side, so he joined Old

Castle Swifts in late 1894 where he was a first team regular until the club disbanded. He was employed at Thames Ironworks as a Marine Boilermaker and played for the club in its opening season appearing in the F.A. Cup match against Chatham and captaining the team when they played Reading reserves on 2nd November 1895. He also appeared in the West Ham Charity Cup final drawn matches, but not the deciding game. In the second half of the 1895/96 campaign he played for South West Ham on a regular basis, and the following season joined Ilford who were in the Southern League at the time but he managed just six first team appearances. At the turn of the century Jamie resided at 13 Kingsland Road, Plaistow, part of the newly developing Bemersyde Estate.

Walter Parks *born Isle of Dogs, March Qtr 1872*

Another one of a band of East End players who already had experience in local district football before Thames Ironworks FC was born. He played for both Old St Luke's and Castle Swifts before and after their amalgamation, and appeared for Thames Ironworks in the club's F.A. Cup tie v Chatham, but then played mainly in the reserve side until he joined St Luke's where he also played in their F.A. Cup match against Ilford in 1896/97. Like his father before him, Walter was a Commercial Clerk and lived at 23 Stopford Road, West Ham.

Johnny Stewart *born Newcastle upon Tyne, 1872*

Began his football career at local club Old St Luke's in 1892/93. When the club was amalgamated and became Old Castle Swifts he continued to play for them until their demise. Working at Thames Ironworks & Shipbuilding Co. as a ships boilermaker he naturally played for the new club in 1895/96. He appeared in the F.A. Cup tie against Chatham when they were beaten by a far more experienced side by five clear goals, but further appearances were confined to the reserve team. He did however, play in all the West Ham Charity cup matches, gaining a winner's medal. Johnny's usual position was at half back, but he played in the forward line in the Charity Cup matches and was commended for his performances. In 1896/97 he had just one first team outing against Leyton in an Essex Senior Cup tie which was lost 2-3. Johnny lived at 67 Malmesbury Road, Canning Town.

A. Williams

Signed from Dartford where he had been captain in 1894/95. Played at least twelve times in Thames Ironwork's initial season, once as captain in a 4-0 victory over the Grenadier Guards. He also appeared in the club's first ever F.A. Cup tie against Chatham. He could play equally well at full back or centre half. Continued playing for the first few weeks of the 1896/97 season but then returned to Dartford to assist them in their first season in the Second Division of the Southern League.

F.A. Cup 1895/96

12. 10. 1895 Chatham (A) 0-5
Att. 3000
Watson , Tull, Williams, Stewart, French, Parks, J. Woods, Sage, Lindsay, Freeman, Darby

West Ham Charity Cup 1895/96

15. 02. 1896 Park Grove (A) 1-0
Result annulled after protest over ineligible players

07. 03. 1896 Park Grove 3-0
Played at St Luke's, Beckton.
Graham, Tull, French, Woods, Williams, Hickman, Chamberlain, Sage, Stevenson, Stewart, Chapman
Scorers:- Stevenson 2, OG 1

21. 03. 1896 Barking 2-2
Final at Spotted Dog. Att. 3000
Graham, Lindsay, French, Woods, Williams, Hickman, Barnes, Sage, Stevenson, Stewart, Chapman
Scorers:- Stevenson, Stewart

28. 03. 1896 Barking 0-0
Replay at Spotted Dog
Graham, Lindsay, French, Woods, Williams, Hickman, Barnes, Sage, Stevenson, Stewart, Chapman

20. 04. 1896 Barking 1-0
2nd Replay at St Luke's, Beckton. Att. 3000
Graham, Stevenson, French, Woods, Chapman, Hickman, Chamberlain, Sage, Freeman, Barnes, Stewart
Scorer:- Barnes

Friendly matches 1895/96

07. 09. 1895 Royal Ordnance Res. (H) 1-1

14. 09. 1895 Dartford Res. (H) 4-0

28. 09. 1895 Manor Park (H) 8-0

05. 10. 1895 Streatham (A) 3-0

19. 10. 1895 Erith Utd (H) 1-2

26. 10. 1895 Old St. Stephen's Res. (H) 4-0

02. 11. 1895 Reading Res. (H) 2-3
Gibson, Jas Taylor, Stevenson, Gillies, Williams, J Woods, Gresham, Chapman, Lindsay, McArthur, W. Barnes
Scorers:- untraced

09. 11. 1895 2nd Grenadier Guards (H) 4-0
Gibson, Taylor, French, Gillies, Williams (c), Woods, Chapman, Gresham, Stevenson, Barnes, Sage
Scorers:- untraced

16. 11. 1895 Charlton Utd (H) 4-0
Gibson, Taylor, Lindsay, Gillies, Williams, Woods, Chapman, Gresham, Stevenson, Barnes, Sage
Scorers:- untraced

23. 11. 1895 West Croydon (H) 2-0
Gibson, Gillies, Williams, Collins, Freeman, Barnes (6 players only traced)

30. 11. 1895 Coldstream Guards (H) 3-1
Gibson, Gillies, Williams, Collins, Dove, Barnes (6 players only traced)

07. 12. 1895 Dartford (A) 0-2
Gibson, Stevenson, Taylor, Gillies, Williams, Collins, Woods, Sage, Dove, Chapman, Gresham

14. 12. 1895 Millwall Res. (A) 0-6
Gibson, Stevenson, Taylor, Morton, Collins, Gillies, Woods, Sage, Dove, Chapman, Gresham

16. 12. 1895 Old St. Stephen's (H) 3-1
(By electric light)
Graham, Taylor, Stevenson, Gillies, Williams, Collins, Sage, Dove, McArthur, Chapman, Gresham
Scorers:- Collins, Dove 2

21. 12. 1895 2nd Grenadier Guards (H) 1-4

25. 12. 1895 South West Ham (H) 4-1

26. 12. 1895 Wandsworth (H) 5-1

28. 12. 1895 Lewisham St. Marys (H) 7-1

04. 01. 1896 Novocastrians (H) 6-1
Graham, Stevenson, Taylor, French, Collins, Morton, Chapman, Gresham, Dove, Woods, Sage
Scorers:- untraced

18. 01. 1896 Upton Park (H) 2-1
Graham, Stevenson, Taylor, French, Collins, Morton, Chapman, Gresham, Dove, Nichols, Woods
Scorers:- untraced

20. 01. 1896 Barking Woodville   (H)   6-2
(By electric light)
Graham, Taylor, Hurst, Morton, Collins, Woods,
Stevenson, Sage, Dove, Chapman, Nichols
Scorers:- Dove 3, Stevenson 2, Nichols

25. 01. 1896 Civil Service   (H)   5-0

01. 02. 1896 Manor Park   (H)   7-2

06. 02. 1896 Royal Ordnance   (H)   2-1
(By electric light). Att. 3000
Graham, Taylor, Hurst, Morton, Collins, Woods,
Stevenson, Sage, Dove, Gresham, Chapman
Scorers:- Sage, Dove

08. 02. 1896 Hornsey   (H)   4-0
Graham, Taylor, Hurst, Morton, Collins, Woods,
Stevenson, Sage, Dove, Gresham, Chapman
Scorers:- untraced

17. 02. 1896 Vampires   (H)   1-3
(By electric light)
Graham, Taylor, Hurst, Hilton, Dove, Gresham,
Stevenson, Chapman, Morton, Woods, Farrell
Scorer:- Gresham

22. 02. 1896 St Luke's   (H)   1-0
Att. 2000
Graham, Taylor, Hurst, Morton, Collins, Woods,
Stevenson, Sage, Dove, Gresham, Chapman
Scorer :- Stevenson

29. 02. 1896 Reading Res.   (A)   2-4
Att. 800
Graham, Taylor, Hurst, Morton, Collins, Hilton,
Woods, Lindsay, Dove, Gresham, Chapman
Scorers:- Woods, Gresham

07. 03. 1896 Fulham   (H)   5-1
Woodford, Taylor, Hurst, Morton, Collins, Hilton,
Farrell, A N Other, Dove, Gresham, Freeman
Scorers:- Gresham 2, Farrell, 2 untraced

09. 03. 1896 West Croydon   (H)   5-0
(By electric light)
Graham, Taylor, Hurst, Morton, Collins, Woods,
Stevenson, Sage, Dove, Gresham, Chapman
Scorers:- Chapman 2, Gresham 2, Stevenson

14. 03. 1896 St Luke's   (A)   1-3

16. 03. 1896 Woolwich Arsenal   (H)   3-5
(By electric light). Att. 2000
Graham, Taylor, Hurst, Morton, Collins, Woods,
Stevenson, Stares, Fitzjohn, Gresham, Chapman
Scorers:- Gresham 2, Fitzjohn

20. 03. 1896 West Bromwich Alb.   (H)   2-4
(By electric light). Att. 1000
Graham, Taylor, G. Neil, Morton, Collins, Stares,
Fitzjohn, Sage, Stevenson, Gresham, Chapman
Scorer:- Chapman 2

28. 03. 1896 Leyton   (H)   3-0

30. 03. 1896 Royal Ordnance   (H)   0-4
Graham, Catling, Hurst, Morton, Collins, Stares,
Woods, Fitzjohn, Stevenson, Gresham, Chapman

03. 04. 1896 St Luke's   (H)   1-1
(Good Friday). Att. 2000
Graham, Neil, Hurst, Morton, Collins, Woods,
Dove, Sage, Stevenson, Gresham, Chapman
Scorer:- Chapman

04. 04. 1896 Liverpool Casuals   H)   3-1
Graham, Williams, Hurst, Morton, Collins,
French, Rossiter, Dove, Stevenson, Gresham,
Chapman
Scorers:- Rossiter, Stevenson, Chapman

06. 04. 1896 Vampires   (H)   6-2
Graham, Hurst, Catling, Stares, Collins, Morton,
H. Rossiter, C. Rossiter, Fitzjohn, Sage, Chapman
Scorers:- untraced

11. 04. 1896 Commercial Ath.   (H)   3-1

18. 04. 1896 South West Ham   (H)   3-0
Graham, Catling, Hurst, Morton, Collins, Stares,
Dove, H. Rossiter, Fitzjohn, Patterson, Gresham
Scorers:- Gresham 2, OG 1

25. 04. 1896 Millwall Res.   (H)   1-1
Graham, Stevenson, Hurst, Woods, Collins,
Stares, Sage, Dove, H. Rossiter, Chapman,
Gresham
Scorer:-Rossiter

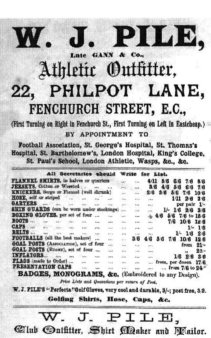

CHAPTER THREE
AWAY FROM HOME
1896/97

One of the most basic, but one of the most important crafts in the shipbuilding yard is that of the riveter, working on the exterior of the ship, hammering home the rivets supplied by the catch-boy and holder-on operating inside the hull. The powerful mallet-type hammers used in the process are depicted in the form of a cross and are enshrined on the club badge which has become synonymous with Thames Ironworks and West Ham United, but although this activity with its incessant noise and perpetual shower of sparks, is the most identifiable operation associated with shipbuilding, it is easy

Workmen at the Thames Iron Works, 1889

to forget that there was a large body of men, each with their own particular skill working as a team to construct large ocean-going vessels.

From the contract, ordering and drawing office stage, work went on site to the carpenters, iron & brass foundrymen, joiners, coppersmiths, anglesmiths, drillers, painters, plumbers, blacksmiths, fitters, apprentices and labourers, not forgetting boilermakers who also used the hammer as their main tool with its unceasing 'tap, tap, tap' during the course of their labours.

It was from this energetic workforce that Thames Ironworks FC drew upon to make up its team, and any players brought in from outside, with just a couple of exceptions for full professionals later on, were obliged to work at the yard.

For the 1896/97 season, with the exciting prospect of entry into the London League and the London Senior Cup, just a few extra players were added, notably Johnny Morrison who had assisted South West Ham the previous season, Fred Chalkley from Park Grove, Edward Hatton from Reading along with Frank Dandridge and Peter Davie.

The campaign kicked off with two friendly fixtures, the second of which was a match against Chatham, their F.A. Cup opponents from the previous season. This resulted in what turned out to be their heaviest defeat in their five-year history, an unbelievable drubbing by 0-9. Apparently the Irons did not play as badly as the score suggests, for every attack that the home side made resulted in a goal! Obviously Graham, the goalkeeper, had a nightmare and was dropped for several games. Dandridge on his debut, was also given the run-around, but kept his place, proved himself and missed only a handful of matches for the remainder of the season.

When the idea of the new London League was first mooted Ted Harsent, Thames Secretary, also wanted the other local clubs, South West Ham and St Luke's, to be admitted because he said 'it would have been better for the game in Canning Town.' Arnold Hills would have agreed, being quite content to stabilize the club's position and enable his workers to benefit from healthy competition on an amateur level. It suggests the more insular outlook that the Ironwork's club had at this time. The committee may have been ambitious in the sense of joining a league and entering senior cup competitions but it would take a further two years for the club to nourish thoughts of professionalism and existing side by side with the 'big guns' of the football world.

Thames first ever league encounter followed on from the previous week's debacle against Chatham when the club entertained Vampires in London League match at Hermit Road. Surprisingly, the committee kept faith with the same team with the exception of Graham, the goalkeeper, who was dropped. Their faith was justified when a 3-0 victory was obtained with Gresham and Morrison the pick of the forwards and Stevenson outstanding in defence.

It is of interest that the local press were now referring to the team as the 'Ironworkers', 'Ironmen' and more often than not the 'Ironsides'.

Once again the F.A. Cup brought no joy when Thames visited another Kent side in this competition, Sheppey United. With the fourth different goalkeeper on duty they suffered another huge defeat, this time by eight clear goals. Southwood, the 'keeper concerned, never played again, being at fault for several of the goals, but the Irons, to be fair, lost Hatton through injury and played most of the game with ten men.

Just two days before, on the 8th October 1896, the club played the Scots Guards in the London League, winning 2-0 at the Hermit Road Ground. This was to be the last time that the first team would ever play at this venue, although they were not aware of it at the time.

There was a very good reason for this, for the Hermit Road Ground was not owned by Thames Ironworks but leased from the Council. Alderman Bethell, who had formerly been the Mayor of West Ham, had succeeded in securing the land as a public recreation ground and the football club was requested to move all their fencing and other property and vacate the land in order that it could be conveyed to the Council. This was duly carried out, but it left the club 'high and dry' without a home ground*. When this was discussed with Alderman Bethell it was alleged that, in his anxiety to compensate the club for the loss of their ground, he gave permission for them to use a piece of land in Beckton Road at the back of the Board School (now the Hardie Primary School adjacent to Fife Road). Believing endorsement had been given, the football committee had to work fast. They engaged 30 men to work for three weeks, firstly to remove the high fencing and all their equipment from Hermit Road, transport it to the new site, sink and concrete the fencing posts deeply into the ground, erect the goal posts, and put up a pavilion. In actual fact the ground had originally belonged to the wife of a Town Councillor, who had transferred it to her brothers. Their agent, most probably on a 'tip off' visited the spot and was alarmed to see this body of men hard at work. This was reported to Messrs Atkinson, the two brothers, who wasted no time in taking the matter to Court.

A summary of the Court proceedings that resulted from these events raises a question or two about the whole affair. The plaintiffs in the case were the Atkinsons, with the defendants being Mr Arnold Hills, Managing Director of Thames Ironworks & Shipbuilding Co., Mr Francis Payne, the honorary secretary of the Thames

The actual site of the Hermit Road football ground was located in the area which is now bordered by Ladysmith Road and Kimberly Road and lies on the west side of Hermit Road. It eventually transpired that only the area on the east side was taken up for the public recreation ground whilst the location where the Irons played was sold off as surplus land for housing.

Ironworks Athletic club, and Alderman Bethell. The plaintiffs complained that the defendants had, without their permission, fenced in the land, constructed a pavilion and goals and advertised football matches on the ground. By way of defence it was said that the land, amounting to over ten acres, had for some years been open and waste ground, which was also used for shooting rubbish upon and that they had obtained permission from Mr Bethell, who had originally been employed by the plaintiffs as their agent for the sale of the land, and the club believed this still applied.

Before the case proceeded, the judge asked the plaintiff's council, Mr Renshaw, what part Mr Hills had taken in the matter. Mr Payne made a statement that Mr Hills was the person who was finding the money for carrying out the works. Mr Renshaw stated that where 30 men were employed for three weeks and a lot of materials were being needed, somebody must have been finding a considerable amount of money. Mr Renshaw then continued 'But I do not want to keep Mr Hills here. He has sworn he has nothing to do with it, and is not finding the money......' He then proposed that Mr Hills be dismissed, and that he should not be personally liable for any costs.

This was agreed, but it should be considered that if Mr Arnold Hills was not aware what had been going on, and did not fund the money for the move and the subsequent work, then who did? If it were Mr Payne's responsibility, being secretary of the Athletics Club, then the money would still have come indirectly from Mr Hills. It would not have come from Francis Payne's pocket.

As to the remainder of the hearing Mr Norton, for the defendants, stated that as soon as the plaintiffs issued a writ and moved for an injunction, the defendants said they would not use the ground, but agreed that at the moment they were trespassers as they still had the fence there, simply because the plaintiffs would not let them take it away.

Then Mr Renshaw caused some laughter in court when he said 'I understand there are some bottles of whisky there.' If Mr Arnold Hills was still in court he would not have seen the funny side of those comments, to put it mildly, considering his never-ending battle with the 'evils of drink.'

Mr Norton then replied that he thought there were some baskets still there, which he asked his Lordship to be allowed to take away. He suggested that Bethell and Payne had both made honest mistakes, and that once told that they had no intention of playing. In respect of the plaintiff's action he then continued 'We promised not to play, and that is not denied. And then they come and put us to all this expense. I have asked my friend and he says he will let me take away the loose things.' Mr Renshaw agreed and replied '....he must have his whisky and mineral waters...'

Mr Norton said once again 'We do not want to play, we only want the fence away. We have another ground and we want to put the fence around it. I do not quite see my friend's position, when he says I am a trespasser, and he will not let me take away the fence which causes the trespass.'

Mr Renshaw then suggested that if the defendants would make a bona fide offer to put an end to the matter on reasonable terms, it would be accepted and if all agreed the injunction would not go ahead.

The judge stated that the defendants would have to pay something and suggested that they offer a sum to cover costs, damages and have liberty to remove their things, and added that he hoped the plaintiffs would be reasonable, but he would have to grant an injunction against Payne and Bethell until a trial or a further order.

Eventually agreement was reached as to costs and therefore no trial took place, but it is interesting to note that the whole action was dismissed against Arnold

Hills, leaving questions remaining. Why did Francis Payne make a statement that Mr Hills paid for the work to be carried out? And why did the Managing Director later refute it? After all, over five years Arnold Hills sunk a lot of money into Thames Ironworks FC and the other social clubs in his organisation over a longer period, not least the building of the Memorial Grounds in 1897.

Of course it is likely that he was completely unaware that the owners of the land in question had not given permission for it to be used for such a purpose, and therefore he would have supplied the finances for the necessary work to be carried out. As soon as it had been realised that the law had been broken, it would have been unwise for him to admit to any collusion in the matter, as he was a man of integrity who had not only funded his Company's Social & Athletic club, but had assisted charities from his own pocket, had organised and paid for Christmas festivities for the children of the poor and had in 1893 founded and financed the 'Ideal Club', which was an organisation set up to meet the social requirements of young men and women engaged in business in London. For Arnold Hills to be hauled through the courts for what, to him, was a relatively unimportant matter would have put a severe dent in his reputation.

As it was, it was left to Bethell and Payne to shoulder the costs, a fact that men concerned with the Ironworks Federated Clubs felt quite indignant about. It is not recorded how those costs were paid, but it is fairly certain that Arnold Hills would have indirectly and discreetly paid them himself. The whole matter, in a very short time, appears to have been conveniently forgotten or 'swept under the carpet' and has remained as hidden history until now.

For Francis Payne, whose hard work, enthusiasm and loyalty were never in question, this would not be the last time that he would be involved in an undertaking that did not go according to plan, but on the next occasion bad judgement would bring his own integrity into question.

It was stated at the hearing that Thames had found a new ground and needed to enclose it, but in the meantime the club played three matches on opponent's grounds and South West Ham also gave permission to use their ground at Tidal Basin for a South Essex League fixture against Woodford. After a 2-0 victory Thames decided to withdraw from that competition due to their ground problems at that time.

Of the three other matches played away prior to appearing on a new home ground, Crouch End were beaten 1-0 in a London League game, Marcians were dumped out of the London Senior Cup 4-0 on November 7th (which followed a victory in same competition against West Norwood in October) and Ilford were held to a 2-2 draw in an exciting London League fixture, after the game had begun 25 minutes late. The home team's equalising goal came due to the ball passing between Graham's legs and maybe as a result of this error the goalkeeper was dropped. He had been more or less a regular since the club's early days, but he did not play again in the first team.

The club had by now found a new home. It was situated at the junction of Byron Avenue and Browning Road, East Ham (which was a country lane at the time), near to the railway station and a distance of about five miles from their original headquarters. In 1896 this was a huge undeveloped area, and Arnold Hills, believing this to be the ideal spot, originally intended to build a large sporting arena there, with an up-to-date running track, a pavilion, stands and terracing. The Ironwork's first game there resulted in a defeat in the Essex Senior Cup against Leyton 2-3 before a good attendance.

Although knocked out of the County Cup at the first hurdle, Thames were going well in the London League, had the West Ham Charity Cup to defend and were still involved in the London Senior Cup, having won through two rounds. Their next opponents in this competition were Wandsworth, who arrived late for the match, but had been held up due to fog. The 'Ironsides' took them apart and were leading 7-0 after 80 minutes play, with Charlie Dove on a hat-trick when the referee abandoned the match due to the increasing bad light. Thames were rightly annoyed that the result would not be allowed to stand, but Wandsworth, having had a very difficult journey due to the weather, did at least turn up, and the rematch was scheduled for the following Saturday. A victory was gained, albeit by a smaller margin, but the worrying thing was that the attendance was a mere 250 spectators.

The result of the match meant that the Ironworks were drawn to meet Barking Woodville at home the following week. The attendance, considering the opponents were 'just down the road', was a disappointing 600 and a large number of those must have been Woodville supporters, because there was a hostile demonstration against the referee at the end of the match in which Thames were victorious by 2-0. The reason for their anger was that two of their team had been ordered from the field. Alf Chalk was dismissed for continual foul play, and 'Sunny' Chalk for abusive language to the referee. In addition, one of the linesmen, Mr Barnett, who was a Barking man and Mr Dixon, the Barking secretary encroached upon the field of play and obstructed the referee in his duties. To cap it all, the Woodville team generally made use of offensive remarks to the referee.

The London F.A subsequently dealt with the matter and the linesman was severely censured with the Barking Woodville secretary suspended from duty for a fortnight. As for the players, 'Sunny' Chalk received a long suspension, but Alf Chalk, due to his reputation, it was said, avoided any punishment. Alf, who was born in Plaistow and then moved to Barking, was employed as a railway clerk. His claim to fame, had it been properly recognised, was that just over three years later he was to be a member of the Upton Park team that represented Great Britain and beat France in Paris in the 1900 Olympic football tournament final.

As far as Thames were concerned the club was through to the next round, but the attendance of 600 was once again a disappointment especially as Barking Woodville brought the majority of that number.

It took four consecutive Saturdays to decide whether Thames Ironworks or Bromley were to go any further in the London Senior Cup. On 23rd January 1897 the tie was postponed. The following week in a titanic struggle at East Ham, the game was abandoned shortly before the end of extra time due to bad light, with the score at 3-3 and although Stares scored another goal at that time, the referee disallowed it. The replay resulted in another draw after extra time at 2-2, but with Bromley winning the toss for choice of home venue, the Kent club also won the second replay by 2-0.

One week later the Irons played Claremont Athletic in their first defence of the West Ham Charity Cup. Hard work was made of this victory as their opponents didn't succumb until the last seven minutes of the game when Thames scored two goals, both from the result of scrimmages. The most intriguing element of the afternoon was not so much the match itself, but the fact that the battleship 'Fuji' which was launched at the Thames shipyards the previous year, was back for some additional work to be carried out, and a group of some 200 Japanese seamen and firemen had been invited along to witness the match. It was said that they were 'especially amused whenever any heavy charging took place.'

Apparently some of them were intending to introduce the game to Japan when they returned, although they were obviously not aware that the game had already been initiated there in 1873. The Japanese took the British Navy as its role model for the Imperial Navy and asked the British Government to send officers to perform naval training. A mission, led by Lt Cdr Archibald Douglas went to Japan and among other activities he introduced competitive sports, including football. It is obvious however, that it did not become established and its history in that country up to the latter half of the 20th Century is a pretty barren one. The national side took part in the Far Eastern Games in 1917 and were beaten 0-15 by the Philippines, and they had almost the worst record in the 1956 Asian Games. It was not until the approach of the 1964 Olympic Games, which were held in Tokyo, that the authorities hired a German coach to assist the national side in the Games. Although they were not successful their performances improved, interest was aroused and in 1965 amateur leagues sprang up. The biggest leap forward was the introduction of the professional J League in 1993 with good class foreign players in the club ranks. This league has now expanded with extra divisions albeit with clubs that do not possess the finances of those in the top J League.

Further progress was made by the Ironworks in the West Ham Charity Cup when the club defeated Manor Park in the semi-final by 2-0. They were then matched against Canning Town side West Ham Garfield in the final at the Spotted Dog. The 'man of the match' was the 'Gar's keeper Bob Heath, for his remarkable shot stopping was the main reason why the 'blue and whites' defeated Thames by a solitary goal. His performance that day, and his general form for West Ham Garfield in the first half of the following season saw the Irons signing him in late January 1898. Garfield appear not to have had a settled home venue at the time and played many matches on away grounds. Once the Memorial Grounds were up and running in 1897/98 Arnold Hills granted them the use of the ground when it was conveniently available and this was still the case at the turn of the century.

A few weeks before the West Ham Charity Cup final, Thames Ironworks had found a new home for their Federated Clubs (Athletic & Social Clubs). These new premises were situated adjoining Canning Town Public Hall, and were opened before

The headquarters of the Thames Ironworks Federated Clubs in Barking Road (on the right, with bow window)

a crowded gathering inside with a presentation to Mr Francis Payne, described as 'the indefatigable worker connected with the Federated Clubs and who is primarily responsible for the existence of the Federation.' There is no doubt the Payne was highly respected by Arnold Hills, despite the contradictions and the fiasco over the trespassing case in Court. The Chairman outlined both problems and successes in the past at the Works, and his high hopes for the future, and then proceeded to give great acclaim to Francis Payne: *'Ten years ago......I found a loyal supporter in Mr Payne. His work was a prelude of what he had done since the bringing out of the social and sporting instincts of the yard. With regard to the various clubs ... no one would deny that the backbone of these new developments was the man they had met to honour that evening. As children they were taught to sing 'Here we suffer grief and pain.' He thought that evening they might sing 'Here we joy to greet Frank Payne.'* Praise indeed.

Arnold Hills then went on to announce that he hoped that by Queen Victoria's accession day in June 1897 to open *'the largest cycle track in London where they would hold such monster meetings that the attention of the Metropolis would be called to the Thames Ironworks.'*

That statement referred to the area just north of Hermit Road, which had already been procured and would be known as the Memorial Grounds. It also meant that the football club's current ground at East Ham would be vacated at the end of the season. Poor attendances and the distance from the Company's headquarters convinced Hills that the present site was not the best option for a new sporting venue and there was a need to return closer to home. It is interesting to note that in his address he referred to the 'cycle track' rather than the 'football stadium'. It indicates that whilst the football club was still an amateur outfit at this stage, it was not considered any more important than any of the other athletic clubs within the Works. When the club did turn openly professional at the onset of the 1898/99 season, Arnold Hills would, of necessity have to plough more funds into it than any other section of his Federated Clubs. It would then be the beginning of a long and memorable journey for the eventual West Ham United, but prove to be the beginning of the end for Thames Ironworks FC.

The evening however, belonged to Francis Payne as more praise was heaped upon him. He was presented with a 'framed address and gold chronometer' and, for his wife, a silver coffee service. In reply to Mr Hills kind words, Payne stated that *'Work had been robbed of its drudgery, and made a pleasure by reason of the kind support he had received ... He had dreamt ... of the good days to come which were to follow the evil ones ... if he could serve the Federated Clubs better in the future he hoped to do so.'* The remainder of the evening was spent with music and singing.

Considering it was Thames' first season in any league a creditable second place in the table had been achieved, with the club finishing just three points behind the eventual London League champions, the 3rd Scots Guards. With a new and spacious home ground for the next season, the future looked bright.

Nobody can deny that the Victorians were first class builders and engineers, and Arnold Hills made no false predictions when he stated that in February 1897 that a brand new stadium would be completed by the anniversary of the Queen's accession in June. Within 14 weeks what had originally been an open field, was now an enclosure with a cycle track fully banked at the corners, with the banking 9ft 6in higher than the inside edge. The surface was of cement, one and a half inches thick laid on concrete of 8 inches thick with a solid foundation of tons of ballast mixed with a small proportion of mould or loam. The track distance was three laps to the mile.

Before all this could be completed, a great deal of heavy work had to be carried out. The soil had to be dug, excavated, removed and re-banked. An area of over four acres was turfed for football, cricket and lawn tennis. A grass margin of 2ft 6 in width was placed around the inside edge of the cycle track with a cinder track 18ft wide running parallel. Great care was taken with drainage as thousands of 2in, 4in, 6in and 9in gullies were used. Terracing was extended all round the track for spectators that would be capable, it was said, of holding an estimated 100,000* people. A red brick pavilion on the home straight had also been constructed to accommodate 1,000 people. Under this stand was a large refreshment room at one

---

* In 1903, the West Ham United Secretary, Lew Bowen, wrote to the F.A who inspected the Memorial Grounds with a view to holding a semi or an F.A Cup Final there. 'I think,' he stated, 'that we have fairly proved the possibilities of putting a crowd of over 100,000 in the Grounds. I believe the correct figures are 133,000 allowing for 16 inches for each person.'

These figures are not so unbelievable as absurd, where the safety and comfort of spectators appears not to have been fully appreciated. Health & Safety regulations today may be considered too stringent, but had such an event taken place at the time without any reliable safeguards it would have been an extremely uncomfortable and downright dangerous experience.

end, with cloakrooms, dressing rooms and lavatories on the ground floor and a cellar at the other end that contained the 'apparatus' for the shower and baths. On the back straight opposite was a timber pavilion that could hold 1,200 people. There was also ample accommodation provided for cycles.

The total cost of the work came to £20,000, which would equate to approximately £1,000,000 at today's values. Arnold Hills may not have considered this a gamble but it was certainly a huge amount of money to invest in a venture that would eventually rely on too many unforeseen factors to be an unqualified success and sadly the arena never did fulfil its potential.

One of the biggest drawbacks not envisaged at the time of completion was the lack of access to certain sides of the arena particularly on the northern side where the proposed railway station at Manor Road West Ham, did not materialise until January 1901, thereby losing almost four years of extra revenue. Entrance was also restricted on the east side of where the East London cemetery was situated directly adjacent to the Memorial Grounds.

Nevertheless Thames Ironworks had the work completed on time and the company held a gala day for their opening in June 1897 as promised. There was an attendance of 8,000 and a number of dignitaries were also present. Both Mr and Mrs Arnold Hills arrived and the band played 'Rule Britannia' in true Empire style. Mrs Hills was presented with a bouquet of flowers and the Venerable Archdeacon Stevens offered a prayer. Mr Hills then unveiled the dedication tablet and delivered a brief address. A presentation was given to two gentlemen who had been engaged in 'creating the ground and organising the sports.' One was a Mr Samuel Turner who had been at the head of work affairs, and the other was Mr Francis Payne (who else?). For appreciation of the latter's organisation the reward was a marble clock – his second timepiece in four months! He was also handed a silver hatchet that was used to cut a cord, and immediately a large coloured Japanese balloon flew open and twenty-four pigeons sped off into the sky. Simultaneously two new club flags were run up, with a salvo of artillery and the National Anthem from the band, the opening ceremony was over. A full programme of cycling events together with foot and walking races then took place. The christening of the Memorial Grounds was over.

PEN PICTURES

Andrew Cowie *born Lochee Scotland, October 21st 1878*

Came to Thames Ironworks from Dundee Harp. A speedy winger with a tremendous shot, who normally played as an outside left, appeared in just two matches, but on the right flank for the Ironworks, both in the London League at the end of the 1896/97 season. He caused some amusement in his second game when he fell into the back of the net in an unsuccessful attempt to bundle the opposing keeper and ball over the line, but he had the last laugh when he scored the equalising goal in a 1-1 draw with Barking Woodville.

He joined Gravesend United in the Southern League First Division the following season and made 6 appearances for them. 1898/99 saw him making a move to the Second Division of the Football League with Manchester City where he played 11 times, netting on three occasions. A return to London for 1899/1900 in the colours of QPR in the Southern League followed where he scored twice in eleven outings. He was on the move yet again in the next campaign, making it six clubs in five seasons when he joined Woolwich Arsenal, but he did not make a competitive appearance for them.

Alex Duff *born Scotland*

Already an experienced goalkeeper when he signed for Thames Ironworks in 1896/97, Duff began his career between the sticks at Scottish League side Cowlairs in 1890/91 where he made 18 appearances. In 1891/92 he joined fellow league outfit Abercorn, turning out on 20 occasions. The following season it was on to Scottish non-league side Northern before returning to his first club Cowlairs in 1893/94 where besides his 16 appearances he played against Rangers in the Glasgow Cup Final in a narrow 0-1 defeat. The 1894/95 season saw him keep goal on another eleven occasions before he came south, appearing for Old Castle Swifts before their collapse that season. After he had joined Thames Ironworks midway through the 1896/97 campaign he played in 4 London League matches, 9 various cup ties and two friendly matches with varying success. His place however was taken by Dave Furnell in 1897/98 and, possibly because he failed to turn up at Aylesbury for a friendly, he was not chosen again for the first team in a competitive match.

Joseph Hurst *born West Ham, circa 1875*

A tough tackling full back who played in at least 15 matches in the Ironwork's first ever season, including five matches 'by electric light.' Affectionately known as 'Curly' he appeared in the club's first three games of 1896/97 and then joined parish side St Luke's. When that club folded he took up with South West Ham at Tidal Basin and played regularly for them. Joseph was a general labourer and lived at 60 Chargeable Street, West Ham.

William Morton *born Walthamstow, March Qtr 1875*

His first club was the Carpenters Institute at Stratford where he was practically an ever-present in the half back line for two seasons from 1892/93. He joined Ilford for the inaugural season of the Southern League in 1894/95 but made just two appearances for them before joining Old Castle Swifts. He was employed by the GER as a loco engine fitter, but when the Swifts collapsed he joined the Ironworks team and played a large part in their first two seasons. He was, what would now be known as 'a tough tackling midfield player', appearing in at least 18 matches in 1895/96 including all but one of the games 'by electric light' and receiving much praise for his display in the memorable friendly against West Bromwich Albion. In November 1896 he became the first ever Ironwork's player to gain representative honours when he was picked to play for Essex against Suffolk. He notched up 16 appearances in various competitions during that season, but in 1897/98 after playing in an early season friendly game, he fell out of favour and played reserve team matches only.

Charles Read *born Canning Town, circa 1870*

Charles Read's first club was local parish side St Luke's in 1894/95. He was employed in the yard as a labourer but did not get his first team chance until the second half of the 1896/97 season when he appeared at fullback in a London Senior Cup defeat against Bromley in February 1897, but he kept that position the following week when Claremont Athletic were beaten in the West Ham Charity Cup. He was then moved up into the forward line for the next five matches, on three occasions in the London League and twice in the West Ham Charity Cup (including the final), scoring three goals along the way, but he never made another first team appearance. Charles lived at 18 Shipwright Street, close to the River Lea, in an area that is now covered by a Business Park and close to the London Gas Museum.

George Sage *born Woolwich, December Qtr 1872*

Played for his first club Old St Luke's in 1892/93. When they were amalgamated with Castle Swifts in 1894/95 he continued with the new club appearing in the forward line and scoring his fair share of goals. George was already working for Thames as a Boiler Maker and being experienced on the local football scene, he became a member of the Ironworks club in its initial season. He could play in any forward position and made at least 20 appearances in the first team including the F.A. Cup tie at Chatham and five of the matches by 'electric light.' He also gained a winner's medal when the Ironworks won their first trophy, beating Barking in the final of the West Ham Charity Cup. The following season of 1896/97 saw George's first team appearances strictly limited for he played just six first team matches, those being two friendlies and strangely enough, one each in different competitions, the London League, London Senior Cup, Essex Senior Cup and South Essex League. George resided at 51 First Avenue, West Ham.

Robert Stevenson *born Barrhead Scotland, May 10th 1869*

Bob began his career at Third Lanark in the Scottish League in 1892/93 where he made ten appearances. Besides his two goals in 15 starts the following season he appeared in a Scottish Cup semi-final against Celtic which unfortunately resulted in a 3-5 defeat, and he also represented the Scottish League against Sunderland in a benefit match. He was basically a defender, but due to his all round ability, he turned out in a number of outfield positions. He came South at the start of the 1894/95 season, joining Football League Second Division side Woolwich Arsenal, where he made seven league appearances in the early part of the campaign, including one match as captain. He subsequently figured in friendly games only for the Plumstead club, but appeared in a benefit game that was billed as Amateurs v Professionals. Stevenson was in the Pro's side but, it is interesting to note that the match resulted in a victory for the Amateurs by 6-1!

In March 1895, although still on Arsenal's books, Bob assisted Old Castle Swifts, but the club were on the brink of collapse at that time, and after a brief return to Scotland, he returned South and joined Thames in the club's first campaign, where due to his quality and experience he soon became captain. He was a big favourite at the Hermit Road enclosure, for although he was not particularly well built for a defender, what he lacked in weight he made up for in skill. This all round ability made him equally at home in any forward position where he pitched in with at least 8 goals in 24 confirmed appearances in that first season including 4 matches in the West Ham Charity Cup in which he gained a winner's medal. The 1896/97 campaign saw the Ironworks compete in several competitions and Bob played in 16 matches and scored 5 goals.

'Captain Bob' as he became known, was sadly missed when he decided to return to his native Scotland in February 1897. He joined non-league club Arthurlie and was quickly into action within several days of his arrival, in the second round of the Scottish Cup against St Mirren. In 1898 he gained a runners-up medal in the Scottish Cup Qualifying competition when Arthurlie were defeated by East Stirlingshire, and he played in further Scottish Cup games for them until 1901. At the end of the decade he was in England once more training the unofficial London Ladies team for what turned out to be a successful competition in Italy against Rome Ladies.

Walter Tranter *born Middlesbrough, 1875*

Came from Teeside to work as a boilermaker and made his first appearance for the Ironworks on Boxing Day 1896. From then on he missed just a couple of matches over the remainder of the season, playing in 16 first team fixtures. Known as a fearless left back, he was an expert at last-ditch tackles with a liking for pushing up-field to feed his forwards. In 1897/98 the Ironworks won the London League Championship with Tranter appearing in twelve of the sixteen fixtures, those missed being due to injury. He also appeared in two F.A. Cup, two London Senior Cup and at least eleven friendly matches that season. Whilst at the awards ceremony for winning the London League Championship he picked up the Dewar Shield in error, much to everyone's amusement.

In 1898/99 he captained the side to their Second Division Southern League Championship missing only two games of their 22 match programme and he also appeared in the three F.A. Cup matches played. At the start of that campaign Tranter had switched from his usual left back position to a permanent move to right back mainly to accommodate new signings Margeram, the Swanscombe full back, and then

Tommy Dunn (ex-Wolves, Burnley and Chatham). In addition to the Southern League he missed only two out of 16 Thames & Medway Combination matches. After playing such a major part in Thames history it was something of a surprise that he joined Chatham for the 1899/1900 season where he made twenty appearances in their Southern League side, but he returned to Canning Town when Thames Ironworks became West Ham United the following campaign, and played in four early Southern League and two F.A. Cup ties, before suddenly leaving in December 1900 to play in Belfast.

London League 1896/97

19. 09. 1896 Vampires (H) 3-0
T. Barnes, Stevenson, Hurst, Morton, Dandridge, Davie, Dove, Rossiter, Hatton, Morrison, Gresham
Scorers:- Hatton 2, Gresham

08. 10. 1896 1st Scots Guards (H) 2-0
Charsley, Stevenson, Holstock, Bird, Dandridge, Davie, Nicholls, Rossiter, Hatton, Gresham, Morrison
Scorers:- Rossiter, Gresham

22. 10. 1896 3rd Grenadier Guards (A) 1-4
Graham, Stevenson, Holstock, Morton, Dandridge, Bird, Dove, Sage, Hatton, Gresham, Morrison
Scorer:- Sage

24. 10. 1896 Crouch End (A) 1-0
Graham, Stevenson, Neil, Bird, Dandridge, Dove, Rossiter, Williams, Hatton, Davie, Morrison
Scorer:- Hatton

28. 11. 1896 Ilford (A) 2-2
Graham, Chalkley, W. T. Taylor, Morton, Dandridge, Bird, Rossiter, Gresham, Dove, Davie, Morrison
Scorers:- Dove, O. G. 1

27. 02. 1897 Vampires (A) 2-1
Duff, Chalkley, Tranter, Bird, Dandridge, Morton, C. Read, Morrison, Butterworth, Gresham, Dove
Scorers:- Morrison, Butterworth

06. 03. 1897 Ilford (H) 3-2
Att. 1500
Duff, Chalkley, Tranter, Bird, Dandridge, Morton, Read, Morrison, Butterworth, Gresham, Dove
Scorers:- Read 2, Butterworth

13. 03. 1897 Barking Woodville (A) 0-1
Duff, Chalkley, Tranter, Jones, Dandridge, Morton, Read, Morrison, Butterworth, Gresham, Dove

01. 04. 1897 3rd Grenadier Guards (H) 0-5
Charsley, Chalkley, Tranter, Dove, Hickman, Bird, Olivant, Chapman, Gresham, Morrison, Butterworth

03. 04. 1897 Crouch End (H) 4-1
Duff, Chalkley, Tranter, Dove, Dandridge, Bird, A. Cowie, Gresham, Butterworth, Cooper, Olivant
Scorers:- Butterworth 2, Cooper 2

08. 04. 1897 Barking Woodville (H) 1-1
Att. 600
Furnell, Chalkley, Tranter, Dove, Dandridge, Bird, Cowie, Gresham, Butterworth, Cooper, Olivant
Scorer:- Cowie

London League Final Table 1896-97

	P	W	D	L	F	A	Pts
3rd Grenadier Guards	12	9	1	2	32	13	19
Thames Ironworks	12	7	2	3	17	17	16
Barking Woodville	12	6	3	3	20	11	15
Ilford	12	7	1	4	26	14	15
Crouch End	12	4	2	6	14	19	10
Vampires	12	3	1	8	10	28	7
London Welsh	12	0	2	10	9	26	2

London Welsh were suspended near the end of the season and as a result Thames Ironworks were awarded two wins. The 1st Scots Guards withdrew and their record was deleted.

Player appearances:- F. Dandridge 10, Charlie Dove 10, George Gresham 10, Dick Bird 9, John Morrison 9, Fred Chalkley 7, H. Butterworth 6, William Morton 6, Walter Tranter 6, P. Davie 4, Alex Duff 4, Edward Hatton 4, H. Rossiter 4, Bob Stevenson 4, H. Graham 3, A. Olivant 3, Charles Read 3, A. J. Charsley 2, T. Cooper 2, Alex Cowie 2, A. Holstock 2, Joseph Hurst 1, T. Barnes 1, William Chapman 1, David Furnell 1, William Hickman 1, Jones 1, George Neil 1, A. Nichols 1, George Sage 1, W. T. Taylor 1, A. Williams 1.

Goal Scorers :- Butterworth 4, Hatton 3, Cooper 2, Read 2, Gresham 2, Cowie 1 Dove 1, Morrison 1, Rossiter 1, Sage 1, OG 1.

(Appearances and goals totals include the match v 1st Scots Guards)

F.A. Cup 1896/97

10. 10. 1896 Sheppey Utd (A) 0-8
Southwood, Stevenson, Holstock, Bird, Dandridge, Davie, Nichols, Rossiter, Hatton, Gresham, Morrison

London Senior Cup 1896/97

17. 10. 1896 West Norwood (A) 2-1
Att. 1500
Charsley, Stevenson, Dove, Morton, Hickman, Stares, Rossiter, Sage, Davie, Morrison, Gresham
Scorers:- Stevenson (pen), Rossiter

07. 11. 1896 Marcians   (A)   4-0
Graham, Stevenson, Taylor, Bird, Dove, Stares, Rossiter, Gresham, Ridges, Davie, Morrison
Scorers:- Gresham 2, Bird, 1 untraced

02. 01. 1897 Wandsworth   (H)   7-0
(match abandoned after 80 mins. due to fog)
Duff, Chalkley, Tranter, Stares, Dandridge, Bird, Rossiter, Gresham, Dove, Morrison, Stevenson
Scorers:- Dove 3, Rossiter, Gresham, Morrison, Stevenson

09. 01. 1897 Wandsworth   (H)   3-1
(replay). Att. 250
Duff, Chalkley, Tranter,Stares, Hickman, Bird, Rossiter, Gresham, Dove, Morrison, Stevenson
Scorers:- Stevenson 2, Gresham

16. 01. 1897 Barking Woodville   (H)   2-0
Att 600
Duff, Chalkley, Tranter, Bird, Dandridge, Stares, Rossiter, Davie, Dove, Morrison, Stevenson
Scorers:- Dove, Morrison

30. 01. 1897 Bromley   (H)   3-3
(stopped in extra time due to bad light)
Duff, Chalkley, Tranter, Bird, Dandridge, W. Woods, Stares, Gresham, Dove, Morrison, Davie
Scorers:- Dandridge, Stares, Dove

06. 02. 1897 Bromley   (A)   2-2
(replay) (after extra time)
Duff, Chalkley, Tranter, Morton, Dandridge, Bird, Rossiter, Gresham, Dove, Morrison, Darby
Scorers:- Gresham, Morrison

13. 02. 1897 Bromley   (A)   0-2
Duff, Chalkley, Read, Morton, Dandridge, Bird, Rossiter, Gresham, Dove, Morrison, Darby

West Ham Charity Cup 1896/97

20. 02. 1897 Claremont Ath   (H)   2-0
Duff, Chalkley, Read, Morton, Dandridge, Bird, Rossiter, Gresham, Dove, Morrison, Hickman
Scorers:- Both goals from a scrimmage

11. 03. 1897 Manor Park   (H)   2-0
Att. 300
Duff, Chalkley, Tranter, Bird, Dandridge, Morton, Rossiter, Gresham, Dove, Morrison, Read
Scorers:- Dove, Read

20. 03. 1897 West Ham Garfield   0-1
Final at Spotted Dog
Duff, Chalkley, Tranter, Bird, Dandridge, Morton, Stares, Rossiter, Dove, Morrison, Read

Essex Senior Cup 1896/97

05. 12. 1896 Leyton   (H)   2-3
Barnes, Chalkley, Taylor, Morton, W. Woods, Hickman, Dove, Sage, Stevenson, Stewart, Stares
Scorers:- Stevenson, 1 untraced

South Essex League 1896/97

26. 09. 1896 Brentwood   (H)   3-2
Barnes, Stevenson, Holstock, Nicholls, Dandridge, Davie, Rossiter, Dove, Sage, Morrison, Gresham
Scorers:- Gresham 2, Dove

31. 10. 1896 Woodford   2-0
Played at South West Ham
Graham, Stevenson,Taylor, Dove, Williams, Bird, Davie, Rossiter, Hatton, Gresham, Morrison
Scorers:- Gresham, Morrison

Thames Ironworks withdrew from the above league

Friendly Matches 1896/97

05. 09. 1896 Q P R   (H)   2-2
Graham, Hurst, Chalkley, Morton, W. Woods, S. Craig, J. Woods, Chapman, Sage, Morrison, Bailey
Scorers: untraced

12. 09. 1896 Chatham   (A)   0-9
Graham, Stevenson, Hurst, Morton, Dandridge, Davie, Dove, Rossiter, Sage, Morrison, Gresham

12. 12. 1896 Barking Woodville   (A)   3-1
Duff, Chalkley, Taylor, Bird, Dandridge, Hickman, Rossiter, Gresham, Dove, Davie, Stevenson
Scorers:- Gresham 2, Davie

26. 12. 1896 Leyton   (A)   1-4
Duff, Chalkley, Tranter, Hickman, Morton, C. Walker, Gresham, Dove, Stevenson, Morrison, Stares
Scorer:- Morrison

27. 03. 1897 Leyton   (A)   1-4
Att. 750
Charsley, Chalkley, Tranter, Dove, Dandridge, Bird, Olivant, Gresham, Butterworth, Hewitt, Cooper
Scorer:- Butterworth

16. 04. 1897 Sheppey Utd   (A)   1-5
Furnell, Chalkley, Tranter, Woods, Dandridge, Hickman, Older, Gresham, Morrison, Dove, Olivant
Scorer:- Dove

CHAPTER FOUR
A NEW ARENA
1897/98

Season tickets for 1897/98 at the club's new arena were fixed at 5 shillings (25p), with ground admission to individual matches being priced at 4d (1½p). This campaign saw the first suggestion of sham-amateurism as the committee announced that the club would insure players for injury, enabling them to receive accident pay from the insurance company if unable to follow their employment.

Several new signings were made for the start of the season. James Reid, an experienced and prolific goal scorer was signed from Reading; Simon Chisholm, a half back, came down from the Scottish club, Thistle FC of Inverness; Edwards, a left winger from Swindon Town; Percy Mills, a forward originally from Reading and then Gravesend, and Older, a right winger from Northfleet. Robert Hounsell, a centre forward, came a little later from Reading and made a good impression, scoring eight goals in ten London League matches, and appeared in the London Senior Cup and friendly games, but after just two matches the following season he left and joined Fulham.

George Neil, who was later to become Thames secretary, was signed permanently from West Norwood. He was no stranger to the Ironwork's team as he had already made several appearances for the club as a guest player. David Furnell, who had turned out for the Irons in the final two games of 1896/97, was chosen as the regular first team goalkeeper.

After such an auspicious occasion at the opening ceremony at the Memorial Grounds in June, Thames arranged a friendly game with Northfleet of the Southern League on September 2nd 1897 for the club's first ever fixture on this ground.

It is of interest to note some of the comments made in an issue of the 'Sportsman' at the time:- *'It is only reasonable to expect an establishment that employs nearly 5000 people to turn out a very good team of footballers. The Thames Ironworks opened their season yesterday at the Memorial Recreation Grounds......meeting Northfleet. During the past few months some very capable players have found employment in the Works and as a result a very creditable exposition of the game was seen...... When the Ironworks have settled down they will be able to hold their own with the best clubs in the district.'*

If nothing else, the above remarks appear to be a thinly disguised accusation that the club were now operating on a sham-amateur basis, and they were probably correct.

The number of spectators present however, was extremely disappointing, for when the teams appeared there were just over two hundred people present. Maybe the opposition was not a strong enough attraction, or the fact that it was a Thursday evening, or it could have been the weather, for the game began with a strong wind and most of the second half was played in heavy rain. Apparently the practice spins of a few cyclists around the track before the match began created just as much interest as the match itself. This activity became something of a routine as riders took to the track before a match and occasionally afterwards when the light allowed.

When the Irons took the field they were sporting their new colours of blue and white with red stockings. Jimmy Reid proved what a valuable acquisition he was by scoring the first ever goal at the Memorial Grounds and the home side went in at half-time one goal to the good. During the second half there was an absolute deluge, which soaked the players to the skin. The game became a bit of a farce as it was impossible for players to keep a foothold, and with the game reduced to a walking pace Northfleet grabbed an equaliser shortly before the finish, despite some good defensive work, especially from Chalkley.

Although Thames had finished runners-up in the London League the previous season, they were keen to go one better in 1897/98, but little did they realise that the result of their opening match in the competition would prove to be of such vital importance come the end of the campaign. The opposition was Brentford and it was the first time the two clubs had ever met. The attendance figure was much improved, being just below the one thousand mark and the crowd witnessed a very even contest with Furnell in goal performing well in the first half, particularly his 'fisting out.' After the break it was end to end, but a few minutes from time an excellent cross from Edwards was converted by Jimmy Reid to give the Irons a narrow victory.

The following Saturday Thames went on the F.A. Cup trail again having failed to make any progress in the club's first two seasons. Their opponents were Redhill, and a victory was gained at last as Simon Chisholm netted twice and an own goal gave the home side a 3-0 victory. The local 'scribe' was impressed but was strongly critical of Hatton and Reid commenting that *'if they would act a little less selfishly there would be a few more goals flying about.'*

For the second consecutive week Thames were engaged in the F.A. Cup with the Royal Engineers Training Battalion being the visitors. Both Hatton and Reid must have read the criticism in the local press and taken the comments to heart as they both combined well to pile on the pressure from the start, but surprisingly the Army side broke away and took the lead. Hatton however, equalised after 15 minutes with a superb shot, and towards the finish of the game Reid played his part by netting the winner.

Sadly, the dream of progressing any further disappeared when Thames could not get past St Albans in the next round, and they were knocked out of the competition by two clear goals. Hatton and Reid must have either 'acted selfishly' or left their shooting boots at home!

There's an old saying in football, uttered more out of wishful thinking than anything else, which says 'Now we are out of the cup, we can concentrate on the league', but the Ironworks did exactly that. The previous season's London League champions, the 3rd Grenadier Guards, were defeated 1-0, and with Essex rivals Leyton already given a thrashing 4-0 at home, the two sides met again in the return fixture at the end of October. With an attendance at the Memorial Grounds of 2,500 in the first match, that figure was improved upon by an additional 500 at Leyton's new ground with its smart grandstand and press box with the enclosure conveniently situated very close to Leyton Midland Road railway station.

By all accounts the game was exciting one but was spoilt somewhat by some very questionable decisions by the referee. (Nothing ever changes!) After some early give and take, Hird scored with a lightning shot from a pass from Gresham, and then Leyton had a spell where Furnell was called into action with a couple of good saves. Late in the half Hounsell had a good run from midfield and scored the Irons' second goal.

It was after the interval that things began to get a bit rough and Leyton were awarded a penalty, which was converted. The ball was set in motion from the centre circle when the referee suddenly stopped play and ordered Hird from the field. As the offence was not apparent some of the crowd made their feelings felt, and some rough play ensued, but Thames, even with ten men, held their own and scored again through Gresham before the end, making it a comprehensive double over their opponents.

There are always two sides to story, especially where there is even the smallest controversial incident during a match. Local press reporting is, on most occasions, naturally biased towards the local team. Showing two opposing viewpoints illustrates the point, for when the correspondent of the 'West Ham Guardian' reviewed the above match he quoted another (unnamed) newspaper's opinion thus:- *'Why will the Thames Ironworks resort to such shady tactics to ensure victory when every member of the team can play good sound football if he likes? Arthur Russell was so badly used by the Ironworkers......that he has since been confined to his bed under the doctor's orders......This roughness should be checked by the Ironwork's committee if they have any regard for the club's good name.'*

This statement could not go unchallenged and our 'Guardian' scribe offered his viewpoint:- *'Now as a common or garden onlooker, I emphatically deny that the roughness was all on one side. In the opening stages of the game one of the Leyton halves adopted very shady methods, and this in the main was responsible for the greater portion of the objectionable tactics. Then, too, the ordering off of the outside left (*Hird) *was sufficient to drive the team to desperation......'*

At this point it is important to consider certain aspects of 'foul play' at the time. Pushing with the hands, or pulling was not acceptable, but from the earliest days 'charging' was permissible providing it was not violent or dangerous. The definition of a charge was one delivered with the shoulder against an opponent's upper body only, so players were given full licence to intentionally knock an opponent off the ball by such a charge. What is more surprising is that an opponent who was about to, or thought to be about to, receive a pass from a colleague could also legally be obstructed in the same manner. This also meant that 'any player seeking an advantage' (i.e. making a run into space) could receive the same treatment.

From the mid 1890s however, some referees were taking a stricter approach and putting their own interpretation on what was fair or not. As players were penalised in one game and perhaps not in the next, confusion often reigned. This resulted in men being cautioned, or even dismissed for foul and abusive language due to lack of consistency by referees.

It took until 1905 before the Football Association considered that the 'men in the middle' were not only depriving the game of its 'robust and manly appeal' but stoppages were becoming frequent due to obvious disputes, with the flow of the game being disrupted. Referees were then advised that 'charging had always been allowed providing that it was not violent or dangerous'. Although it was not strictly stated it was a request to be a little more flexible in interpretation, which still, of course, left responsibility up to the much-maligned referee! Eventually charging opponents who were not in possession was outlawed, and even a good old-fashioned shoulder charge is rarely seen these days.

However the F.A. underlined the fact that they would support referees in being more stringent in putting down 'rough play' such as 'tripping', 'kicking' and 'jumping' at opponents and 'handling', 'pushing' and 'charging an opponent from behind'.

The following three Saturdays brought three victories for the Irons, two of which were friendly encounters, but the other was a clear cut 3-0 London League victory against Barking Woodville, making it five wins from five matches played in that competition.

On November 27th 1897 the Ironworks met Novocastrians at their Ponders End enclosure in the London Senior Cup. The 'Novos' were unbeaten on their own ground at that time, but the peculiarities of their pitch may have had some bearing on that, for there was a distinct slope from one end to the other with a blanket of long grass covering a bumpy surface. Recent heavy rain caused muddy conditions however, and what with playing uphill against the wind the Irons had to be at their best to keep level until half-time. It was reported that at the start *'...the Ironworks appeared on the field with brand new white spotless clean knickers and light blue shirts, but before they had been playing long they were like blackamoors, to the huge delight of the Novo's spectators.'* After the interval Thames had the last laugh when they were kicking downhill with an even greater wind behind them, and they eventually ran out winners, after going a goal down, by 3-1.

On the Wednesday before the above match Thames had their second representative honour when goalkeeper Dave Furnell was chosen to appear for Essex against Middlesex at Wood Green. Although he had a steady game the Middlesex side were far stronger overall and won by 5-2. Billy Barnes, the ex-Ironworks player scored one of the Essex goals. This was another occasion when transport problems caused a late start when four of the Essex team missed their train at Liverpool Street station. They changed into playing gear on the next available train, but the match had to be reduced to 35 minutes each way. To rub salt in their wounds, the Middlesex side had a tea provided for them by their Association but the Essex team did not, which caused some resentment, for on previous occasions the County team had been entertained in excellent style, but Mr Kirkup, who was in charge of the Essex side said he was authorised to pay for drinks, but not for a meal.

George Neil and Walter Tranter, the Thames full-back partners were the next to receive representative honours the following month when they played for the London League against London F.A. It is not known whether tea was provided!

Thames continued their excellent league form with a 5-1 thrashing of the 2nd Grenadier Guards, but dropped their first point when Ilford held them to an exciting 3-3 draw with Furnell making some first class saves against a rampant Ilford attack. Hird was the Irons best outfield player pitching in with two fine goals.

In between those two matches a friendly game had been arranged with Willesden & Metropolitan Railway FC, but due to injuries sustained against the Guards and in a match against an Arsenal reserve side Dove, Hird, Gresham, Nichol, and Taylor were unable to play. Hounsell and Neil, due to unforeseen circumstances were not able to appear, and Dandridge and Bird had already promised to guest for Southall. So for the first and only time the club took the field and played from the start of a match with only ten men, but still managed a 2-1 victory.

Over the Christmas period Thames had four friendly matches (three wins and one loss) and Victor Ridges made outstanding appearances in goal, although he had been a very popular centre-forward for South West Ham for three seasons, and at the time played up front for the Ironworks reserves.

In the New Year the club continued their impressive league form, scoring 15 goals in three outstanding victories. Whilst Neil and Tranter had a good understanding in defence, Chisholm, Dove and later Gillies controlled the middle with Gresham (as ever), Edwards and Hird the pick of the forwards.

Arnold Hills maintained a personal interest in the Company's football team, as he did with all his clubs and societies, and maybe he had hoped to inspire the team to better things when he penned the following message in typical Victorian style at the start of the 1897/98 season.

'To the players:- As an old footballer myself, I would say, get into good condition at the beginning of the season, keep on the ball, play an unselfish game, pay heed to your captain, and whatever the fortunes of the first half of the game, never despair of winning, and never give up doing your very best to the last minute of the match. That is the way to play football, and better still, that is the way to make yourselves men.'

Simple, but very sound advice that appears to have been heeded as performances and results testified.

The Managing Director, however, had many other matters that were of more concern to him. His never-ending crusade against the evils of drink continued unabated. In December 1897 he occupied the Chair at the Public Hall, Canning Town for a Temperance meeting in favour of Sunday closing. It was the intention to make united attempts to accomplish Sunday closing of all licensed houses in England. Outside of the Temperance Society it was not a campaign that every one agreed upon, but Hills' paternal attitude reached out into other areas of life and his generosity towards good causes knew no bounds. Amongst other contributions he was responsible for a yearly gathering at the Public Hall, Canning Town to give entertainment to 2,000 children of the men employed in the yard. On New Year's Eve 1897 it was reported that *'Professor Anderson gave a few conjuring tricks and the young people were much amused by the comical actions of some of the Thames Ironworks Minstrels. Mr Hills gave a short address, and after nearly two hours had been spent in an enjoyable manner the children were marched out of the hall, each receiving a bun and an orange.'* At the following New Year's event a Punch & Judy show was performed, and it is interesting to note that those acting as stewards included Francis Payne, and players from the Ironworks football team – Collins, George Neil, Victor Ridges and Tommy Dunn. On this occasion, in addition to the bun and the orange, the children received an India rubber ball each!

Those three excellent London League victories were followed by the club's dismissal in the London Senior Cup by Ilford, although Thames had the excuse of being without three of their regular players due to the rules regarding residential qualifications. In addition, David Furnell in goal had a nightmare of a match and this led to the signing of Robert Heath of West Ham Garfield a few days later. David did not appear in the first team again.

The month of February was full of friendly fixtures one of which was away to Queens Park Rangers. In a 1-1 draw the local correspondent expressed his opinion that the *'Ironworks are a well balanced side, solid in defence, with a nippy forward line... Hird is an exceptional player both at dribbling and shooting... Heath made several fine saves, once fisting the ball over.'* There was no doubting that Bob Heath was a good goalkeeper, but it is always a vulnerable position to sustain. When the club began Gibson was the first choice, followed by Graham, but he was then replaced by Duff, who in turn gave way to Furnell, and now Heath was the man 'between the sticks,' but he would be replaced by Tommy Moore the following season when the club turned professional. Competition for positions in football is constant, with goalkeepers especially insecure.

On the final Saturday in February the Irons at last played another London League game, visiting Stanley, who played at Capt. James' private ground at West Brompton. A very tight encounter resulted in a 1-1 draw. The Ironworks football philosophy was the short passing game that was handed down to West Ham United and became a tradition, but on that occasion the ball was in the air and with the Stanley defence of much bigger stature the Irons forwards found little joy in attack, but at least they shared the spoils.

Mention of Stanley reveals an amusing incident between Ilford and Stanley in the same league the week after the above match. The local Ilford correspondent made the following observation:- *'I am not an anti-tobacconist but I do not think it is at all good form for a goalkeeper to be seen smoking a cigarette in goal whilst the game is in progress, and for a linesman to be seen smoking a pipe. Yet both incidents occurred on Saturday at Ilford.'*

Smoking or not, it was Thames who were on fire when they met Bromley in their return league match in Kent. A 5-1 drubbing of the locals on the day, added to the 7-3 home victory earlier in the season, was substantial revenge for the defeat in the London Senior Cup in the previous campaign.

It was said that for this away fixture the visitors came down in four horse-brakes to see the match, and this mode of transport, which was the Victorian equivalent of the present day mini-bus, was often used for teams and supporters for parts of a journey that was not covered by train.

Another 'double' was achieved when the previous year's champions 3rd Grenadier Guards were defeated by 3-1, and with the Ironworks now having obtained the experienced and much admired Arthur Oxspring in defence, there were just two vital matches remaining in the chase for the London League title.

At this stage there were only two clubs in contention with Thames on 25 points and Brentford on 24, with the vital clash between the two to come on April 23rd 1898. With the fixture being away from home, travelling plans to the West London club turned out to be something of an innovation. There was no involvement of horse-brakes on this occasion as a party of two hundred supporters left aboard a boat from the Ironworks wharf around noon and set off along the Thames to Kew. This must have been one of the first, if not the very first occasion that a set of supporters had made a journey by river for an away match in this country. It was certainly appropriate considering the club's shipyard background. From there they boarded a train to Shotters Field to what was described as 'the pretty little town of Brentford.'

There was a great deal of interest in the game as Brentford needed a victory to put them on top, with one match remaining. If the Ironworks won then they would be champions, and with this in mind there was a healthy attendance of 3,000. Naturally, it was a hard fought encounter with end-to-end play, but when Neil, Thames right back, conceded a free kick just outside the penalty area, Lloyd, who was to play for the Irons the following season, headed the ball into the net for the home side. Just before the break Woodcock, the Irons outside left, twisted a knee and took no further part in the match. What with playing a man short and with Hird having a goal disallowed for offside in the second half the Irons knew it was not to be their day, and they suffered their first league defeat of the season. Brentford were now top and had only to beat lowly Barking Woodville in their final match to take the title. Thames had to win against 2nd Grenadier Guards and hope that Brentford would suffer an unlikely defeat.

During the week before that all-important final match the Ironworks arranged a friendly fixture at the Memorial Grounds against a Woolwich Arsenal side that fielded nine regular first team players. The visitors opened the scoring with a very dubious penalty but play was very even, not to say fast and furious, with chances at both ends. As this was an evening fixture and the daylight was fading quickly both teams agreed to the referee's request to turn straight round at half-time and play on, which says much for both team's fitness. (It is not widely realised however, that in those days referees were instructed that the half-time period should not exceed *five* minutes in any case).

The Irons gave a great account of themselves after the 'non-existent' break, and scored twice to lead 2-1 until, with seconds to go, Arsenal grabbed an equaliser. This encounter proved that Thames could compete with the best, as the Woolwich side had finished their Football League Second Division programme in fifth place. Agreeing to play ninety minutes straight off however, was perhaps unwise with such an important league game four days away.

An odd situation arose before that match actually took place, as the 2nd Grenadier Guards at that time were obliged to move barracks to Pirbright in Surrey and it was deemed more important to them to pull out of the fixture and concede the points. As the outcome would decide the title, the London League executive instructed the military outfit that the match had to be fulfilled, although the game, which should have been an away fixture, was switched to the Memorial Grounds. The 2nd Grenadier Guards were a very poor side, bottom of the table with only 3 points and nothing to play for, but to be fair they gave plenty of effort, but Thames had only ten men almost from the start when Dove received a bad injury, but they still ran out easy winners by 3-1.

Communications in those days were not exactly instantaneous like they are today, but when news filtered through that Brentford had amazingly been beaten by Barking Woodville in their final match, the players of Thames Ironworks were overjoyed that they had won their first league title.

1897/98. Players at the back are believed to be Neil, Furnell and Tranter. On the front row, James Reid is second from left and Gresham is second from the right.

PEN PICTURES

Richard Bird *born Hetton Durham, 1869*

Richard's family came south when he was a child and after leaving school he eventually became a Ship's Joiner. 'Dickie' as he was affectionately known, gained a first team place in the club side in 1896/97, where he was an accomplished and reliable half-back throughout that season. He appeared in the first team on 22 occasions including the final of the West Ham Charity Cup, in which Thames were beaten by West Ham Garfield by a single goal. The following campaign began well enough for him, but he eventually made just five appearances in the first eleven, the remainder being played in the reserves. He figured in one first team fixture in 1898/99 at the end of the club's Southern League Second Division championship success in a 2-0 victory over Southall.

Frederick Chalkley *born Plaistow, March Qtr 1875*

Began his football career with Park Grove (Plaistow), where he became captain of the club in 1893/94. He remained with them until he joined the Thames Ironworks club in 1896/97. He was a very steady and competent right back who was selected for the initial Iron's match of that campaign in a friendly against QPR. He had then to earn a permanent place in the first eleven but when he did in November 1896, he did not miss a match for the rest of the season, making 7 appearances in the London League, 6 in the London Senior Cup, 3 in the West Ham Charity Cup and 5 in friendly games. After November 1897 however, he lost his place due to the successful full back partnership of Neil and Tranter, and he was relegated to the second eleven until the end of 1897/98. He then joined London League side Monsteds Athletic and became a firm favourite with them. Fred was a painter by trade and lived at 3 Rochester Avenue, Upton Park, which is just one train stop away from his first club's Park Grove ground which was situated alongside Plaistow railway station in Riles Road (now Stride Road). That club's dressing room was at the nearby Railway Tavern, where smoking concerts were often held after matches.

Simon Chisholm *born Banff Scotland, July 7ᵗʰ 1873*

Simon came from the Inverness Thistle club who were a Scottish non-league side. He played for them in their Scottish F.A. Cup match against Dundee in 1896/97, but in the latter part of that season he made the long trip South to obtain employment at Thames Ironworks. He not only found work as an Engine Fitter at the yard but he

went straight into the football club's first eleven for the 1897/98 campaign where he played in all but one game in the London League Championship winning side. He also figured in four various cup ties and at least eleven friendly fixtures. A tough tackling half back with a good ball distribution he played a vital part in the 1898/99 campaign when Thames won the Southern League Second Division title, appearing 17 times including their Championship decider and Test match. He also played in 3 F.A. Cup ties and 10 Thames & Medway Combination matches. His best position was at left half but when Thames brought in a number of players for the 1899/1900 season he was no longer 'in the frame' mainly due to the signing of Roddy McEachrane. Simon then signed for Barking Woodville in October 1899, but he moved to Kent in 1900 and played for Chatham in the Southern League until that club went into liquidation in 1901. The club rose again however, to play at a lower level administered by a committee.

Francis Cox *born Stratford, 1877*

A half back and occasional winger who played on just two occasions in the first eleven in 1897/98, once in a friendly match, with the other appearance coming in the 7-3 thrashing of Bromley in a London League match, but he also figured in the reserve side that season. He is included here mainly for the interesting fact that he was employed in the shipyard as an Army and Navy gun lights fitter.

David Furnell *born West Ham, June Qtr 1874*

Although better known as a goalkeeper, David spent four seasons as an outfield player, where he was equally useful as a full back or in the half back line. He began his career with Old St Luke's in 1892/93 and he remained with them when they were amalgamated with Castle Swifts. On their collapse he joined parish side St Luke's at Beckton in 1895/96 where he was made club captain. He received a bad leg injury in March 1896 that kept him out of the side for 6 weeks and he was disappointed to be left out of the team that met Thames Ironworks in April, but insisted on 'running the line' in that match. Later that month, eager to return, he guested for Barking, playing for them in goal. When the St Luke's club 'went under' midway through the following campaign he joined Thames Ironworks FC, where he was already employed as a labourer, and he made his first appearance in the final League match of the season in goal giving a creditable show in a 1-1 draw with Barking Woodville. The best feature of his game was his accurate 'fisting out', something which was vital at the time because by holding the ball in the area 'keepers were left vulnerable to being bundled legitimately over the goal line if not protected by a full back. He was first choice 'keeper for 1897/98, giving sound performances and gaining representative honours for Essex against Middlesex in November 1897. Thames however, signed the highly rated Bob Heath from West Ham Garfield in late January 1898, probably recalling his brilliant display in the previous season's West Ham Charity Cup Final, and David lost his place in the first team.

In previous Thames Ironworks and West Ham United publications the above player has often been confused with George Fundell who played as a forward for Old St Luke's in the early 'Nineties and had also had a stint as a referee. George, who was a local businessman, became a Director of West Ham United, being sometime Treasurer and Assistant Secretary. When he died in 1920 his coffin was carried by members of the then current team.

Robert Heath *born Deptford March Qtr 1874*

Robert's first club was the Forest Gate side, St Peters in 1892/93. In November 1892 the club visited Chigwell, and the local press reported that *'The Saints, accompanied by their President, the Rev. A. Durrant, journeyed to Chigwell on Saturday to meet the school XI and a hard fought game resulted in a draw of two goals each...... After the match the visitors were entertained by the Master of the school, and an excellent tea was provided, the visitors being shown around the school gymnasium, and after a pleasant day's outing arrived home about half past seven.'*
Robert joined neighbours Park Grove the following season, being there at the same time as Fred Chalkley. He remained there until 1896/97 when he signed for West Ham Garfield. After outstanding displays he joined Thames Ironworks FC in late January 1898. He was already employed as a shipyard labourer at the Works and by becoming the club's regular 'keeper ironically displaced Dave Furnell, also employed as a labourer at the shipyard. Bob however, was to receive the same treatment when the Irons went professional as Tommy Moore took over, so he moved on to Barking Woodville during 1898/99, followed by two complete seasons with Ilford.

John Morrison *born Scotland, circa 1875*

Johnny, who was a forward, was employed at the Castle Line Works of Donald Currie and began his football career with Old Castle Swifts in 1894/95 and had a good goalscoring record for

them. After the club's collapse he was taken on by South West Ham the following season, but joined Thames Ironworks FC in 1896/97. He played in all competitions making 27 appearances overall scoring 6 goals. Presumably this scoring ratio was not considered good enough and he played in just three matches the following season and did not appear in the first team again.

Arthur Oxspring *born West Ham, Sept Qtr 1875*

Arthur was a big, strong character who was basically a defender with a no nonsense style, but who conversely had a reputation for his footballing skills. He began his career as a youngster at Old St Luke's in 1892/93 and then joined South West Ham the following season. Moving on to Old Castle Swifts in 1894/95, he followed on to Beckton side St Luke's for the next campaign, but was soon back with South West Ham later the same season, where he became captain in 1896/97, but then joined his fifth club when he signed for Thames Ironworks FC in the second half of the1897/98 campaign. He was already employed at the Works as an Iron/Brass Moulder, like his father before him, but after just six first team and two reserve games for the Irons his talented feet were on the march again and he joined up with former South West Ham team-mate, Billy Barnes at Leyton for 1898/99. He was a regular there for two seasons. Arthur resided at 112 Forty Acre Lane, West Ham.

James Reid *born Scotland, circa 1874*

Jimmy was a forward with an excellent scoring record at his first club, Southern League Reading, where in two seasons from 1895/96 he netted 14 goals in 23 appearances. When he became available Thames were quick to acquire his services for the start of the 1897/98 season. He was a valuable member of the side that won the London League title being an ever-present in a programme of 16 matches and contributing 10 goals. That campaign he also played in 3 F.A. Cup ties and a known 15 first team friendlies, scoring at least 5 goals. The following season Jimmy picked up another medal when the Irons won the Southern League Second Division title, with a further haul of 9 goals in 14 matches, and with four goals in 11 games in the Thames & Medway Combination he maintained his above-average goalscoring record. The acquisition of Carnelly, Bradshaw, Joyce and McKay in 1899/1900 however, saw Jimmy squeezed out and he played just 3 matches in 3 different competitions. Even so he scored 3 goals. He was employed as a shipyard timekeeper. Jimmy is not to be confused with his namesake who came from Burslem Port Vale in 1900/01 and played for the new West Ham United club.

Victor Ridges *born Thirley Hampshire, Dec Qtr 1871*

Moved as a child with his family to the local area and began his football career at South West Ham in 1893/94 being a regular in the first team for three seasons. He was a great favourite of the Tidal Basin faithful who admired his swashbuckling style at centre forward. A local report of a match against Ilford in 1896 illustrates the point. *'Again Vic Ridges treated South's supporters to a dashing and well-nigh faultless display at centre as he forced the pace, kept the wings well together and was always dangerous in front of goal.'* He joined the Thames Ironworks club in 1896/97, where he was already employed as an Engineer's Clerk, but he made just one first team appearance that campaign in the London Senior Cup. Travelling with the team in December 1897 to a friendly fixture at Aylesbury, he took over in goal when Duff failed to turn up. He gave such an outstanding performance that after the match he was waited on at the local Bell Hotel and offered the goalkeeping position in the home side, but he politely declined, saying he did not wish to 'migrate' for the present! One week later on Christmas Day, he made another appearance 'between the sticks', but then reverted to his natural centre forward position, although he had to be content with reserve team football. In 1900 he moved to Bury St Edmunds in Suffolk and married a local girl.

London League 1897/98

11. 09. 1897 Brentford (H) 1-0
Att. 1000
Furnell, Chalkley, Dove, Chisholm, Dandridge, Bird, Mills, Gresham, Hatton, Edwards, Reid
Scorer:- Reid

02. 10. 1897 Leyton (H) 4-0
Att. 2500
Furnell, Chalkley, Neil, Dove, Dandridge, Chisholm, Denham, Gresham, Hatton, Reid, Edwards
Scorers:- Hatton, Gresham, Reid 2

23. 10. 1897 3rd Grenadier Guards (A) 1-0
Furnell, Neil, Tranter, Dove, Taylor, Chisholm, Edwards, Hird, Gresham, Reid, Gillies
Scorer:- Reid

30. 10. 1897 Leyton (A) 3-1
Att. 3000
Furnell, Neil, Tranter, Dove, Taylor, Chisholm, Gillies, Reid, Hounsell, Gresham, Hird
Scorers:- Hounsell, Gresham, Hird

13. 11. 1897 Barking Woodville (H) 3-0
Furnell, Neil, Tranter, Dove, Taylor, Chisholm, Nichols, Gresham, Hounsell, Reid, Gillies
Scorers:- Gresham 2, Reid

02. 12. 1897 2nd Grenadier Guards (H) 5-1
Furnell, Dove, Tranter, Gillies, Taylor, Chisholm, Hird, Reid, Hounsell, Gresham, Edwards
Scorers:- Edwards 3, Hird, Gresham

11. 12. 1897 Ilford (A) 3-3
Furnell, Neil Tranter, Dove, Taylor, Chisholm, Hird, Gresham, Reid, Gillies, Edwards
Scorers:- Hird 2, Reid

01. 01. 1898 Ilford (H) 4-0
Furnell, Neil, Tranter, Gillies, Taylor, Hickman, Edwards, Reid, Bone, Gresham, Foss
Scorers:- Reid, Bone, Gresham, OG 1

08. 01. 1898 Stanley (H) 4-2
Att. 600
Furnell, Neil, Tranter, Gillies, Taylor, Chisholm, Hird, Gresham, Hounsell, Reid, Edwards
Scorers:- Gresham 3, OG 1

15. 01. 1898 Bromley (H) 7-3
Furnell, Neil, Tranter, Cox, Chisholm, Gillies, Hird, Edwards, Hounsell, Reid, Gresham
Scorers:- Edwards 3, Hounsell 2, Gresham, Gillies

26. 02. 1898 Stanley (A) 1-1
Att. 3000
Heath, Neil, Tranter, Taylor, Gillies, Chisholm, Hird, Reid, Fitzjohn, Gresham, Edwards
Scorer:- Gresham

12. 03. 1898 Barking Woodville (A) 0-0
Att. 1500
Heath, Neil, Rooff, Chisholm, Taylor, Gillies, Hird, Gresham, Hounsell, Reid, Edwards

19. 03. 1898 Bromley　　　　　(A)　　5-1
Heath, Neil, Rooff, Gillies, Taylor, Chisholm, Hird, Reid, Hounsell, Gresham, Edwards
Scorers:- Reid 3, Hird, Hounsell

02. 04. 1898 3rd Grenadier Guards (H)　3-1
Heath, Neil, Tranter, Dove, Oxspring, Chisholm, Hird, Reid, Hounsell, Gresham, Edwards
Scorers:- Hounsell 2, Neil

23. 04. 1898 Brentford　　　　　(A)　　0-1
Att. 3000
Heath, Neil, Tranter, Dove, Oxspring, Chisholm, Hird, Reid, Hounsell, Gresham, Woodcock

30. 04. 1898 2nd Grenadier Guards (A)*　3-1
* played at Memorial Grounds
Heath, Neil, Tranter, Dove, Oxspring, Chisholm, Hird, Reid, Hounsell, Gresham, Foss
Scorers:- Hounsell 2, Gresham

London League Final Table 1897-98

	P	W	D	L	F	A	Pts
Thames Ironworks	16	12	3	1	47	15	27
Brentford	16	12	2	2	43	17	26
Leyton	16	8	4	4	41	33	20
3rd Grenadier Guards	16	7	3	6	34	33	17
Ilford	16	5	7	4	33	25	17
Stanley	16	5	4	7	22	22	14
Barking Woodville	16	2	6	8	16	37	10
Bromley	16	4	2	10	20	49	10
2nd Grenadier Guards	16	0	3	13	17	42	3

Player appearances:- George Gresham 16, James Reid 16, Simon Chisholm 15, George Neil 14, A. Edwards 12, Henry Hird 12, Walter Tranter 12, Gillies 11, Charlie Dove 10, David Furnell 10, Robert Hounsell 10, W.T. Taylor 10, Bob Heath 6, Arthur Oxspring 3, Fred Chalkley 2, F. Dandridge 2, L. Foss 2, Edward Hatton 2, J. Rooff 2, Dick Bird 1, J.P. Bone 1, F. Cox 1, Denham 1, J. Fitzjohn 1, William Hickman 1, Percy Mills 1, A. Nichols 1, A. Woodcock 1

Goal Scorers:- Gresham 12, Reid 10, Hounsell 8, Edwards 6, Hird 5, Hatton 1, Bone 1, Gillies 1, Neil 1, OG 2

F.A. Cup 1897/98

18. 09. 1897 Redhill　　　　　(H)　　3-0
Att. 1000
Furnell, Chalkley, Tranter, Dove, Dandridge, Chisholm, Older, Hatton, Reid, Gresham, Edwards
Scorers:- Chisholm 2, OG 1

25. 09. 1897 R E Training Battalion (H)　2-1
Att. 1200
Furnell, Chalkley, Tranter, Dove, Dandridge, Chisholm, Older, Hatton, Reid, Gresham, Edwards
Scorers:- Hatton, Reid

16. 10. 1897 St. Albans　　　　(A)　　0-2
Att. 1000
Furnell, Chalkley, Taylor, Dove, Dandridge, Gillies, Hird, Gresham, Hatton, Reid, Edwards

London Senior Cup 1897/98

27. 11. 1897 Novocastrians　　(A)　　3-1
Furnell, Neil, Tranter, Dove, Dandridge, Chisholm, Edwards, Cooper, Hounsell, Gresham, Morrison
Scorers:- Cooper, Hounsell, OG 1

22. 01. 1898 Ilford　　　　　　(H)　　1-3
Furnell, Neil, Tranter, Bird, Dandridge, Chisholm, Morrison, Gresham, Hounsell, Reid, Edwards
Scorer:- Gresham

Friendly matches 1897/98

02. 09. 1897 Northfleet　　　　(H)　　1-1
Att. 200
Furnell, Chalkley, Tranter, Chisholm, Dandridge, Bird, Hatton, Gresham, Reid, Mills, Edwards
Scorer:- Reid

04. 09. 1897 Northfleet　　　　(A)　　0-1
Furnell, Chalkley, East, Morton, Dandridge, Bird, Denham Gresham, Hatton, Reid, Edwards

23. 09. 1897 Millwall　　　　　(H)　　0-2
Att. 1200
Furnell, Chalkley, Tranter, Dove, Dandridge, Chisholm, Denham, Gresham, Hatton, Reid, Edwards

09. 10. 1897 Kettering　　　　(H)　　1-3
Att. 1800
Furnell, Chalkley, Taylor, Dove, Dandridge, Gillies, Older, Gresham, Hounsell, Reid, Mills
Scorer:- Gresham

21. 10. 1897 West Ham Garfield　(H)　3-1
Furnell, Taylor, Tranter, Dove, Gillies, Chisholm, Hird, Gresham, Hounsell, Reid, Cox
Scorers:- Hounsell 2, Reid

06. 11. 1897 2nd Lifeguards　　(H)　　6-0
Furnell, Neil, Chalkley, Hird, Taylor, Bird, Nichols, Gresham, Hounsell, Reid, Gillies
Scorers:- Gillies 2, Gresham 2 (1 a pen), Hird 2

20. 11. 1897 St. Albans　　　　(H)　　2-1
Furnell, Neil, Tranter, Dove, Taylor, Chisholm, Hird, Gresham, Hounsell, Reid, Gillies
Scorers:- Gresham 1pen, Gillies

27. 11. 1897 Woolwich Arsenal Res (H)   1-4
(reserve team match)
Duff, Chalkley, Hickman, Morton, Taylor, Bird,
Nichols, Hird, Hind, Reid, Gillies
Scorer:- Gillies

04. 12. 1897 Willesden & Metroplitan Rly (H) 2-1
Furnell, Hind, Tranter, Gillies, Morton,
Chisholm, Edwards, Reid, Cooper, Morrison
(only ten men played)
Scorers:- Cooper, 1 untraced

18. 12. 1897 Aylesbury Utd   (A)   2-1
Ridges, Jas Taylor, W. Taylor, Morton, Hickman,
Hind, Foss, Nichols, Bone, Hird, Gillies
Scorers:- Foss, Gillies

25. 12. 1897 South West Ham   (H)   4-0
Ridges (g), Dove, Bone, Gresham, Reid, Gillies
(only six players traced)
Scorers:- Gillies 2, Bone, Reid

27. 12. 1897 Barking Woodville   (A)   0-1

28. 12. 1897 2nd Grenadier Guards (H)   4-0

20. 01. 1898 Ferncliffe   (H)   4-1

29. 01. 1898 Commercial Ath   (H)   1-2
(reserve team match)
Knight, Oxspring, McDougall, Morrison, Morton,
Hickman, Rossiter, Mills, Ridges, Bone, Cox
Scorer:- untraced

03. 02. 1898 Upton Park   (H)   3-1

05. 02. 1898 Gravesend   (A)   1-4
Heath, Neil, Tranter, Hind, Taylor, Chisholm,
Hird, Gresham, Hounsell, Reid, Gillies
Scorer:- Hounsell

12. 02. 1898 Q P R   (A)   1-1
Heath, Neil, Tranter, Chisholm,Taylor, Hickman,
Hird, Reid, Hounsell, Gresham, Gillies
Scorer:- Reid

19. 02. 1898 New Brompton   (H)   2-2
Heath, Neil, Tranter, Barker, Taylor, Chisholm,
Hird, Reid, Fitzjohn, Gresham, Gillies
Scorers:- Chisholm, Gresham

05. 03. 1898 Woolwich Arsenal Res. (H)   3-1

12. 03. 1898 Clapton Reserves   (H)   2-1
(reserve team match)
Knight, A N Other, Chalkley, Morton, Barker,
Furnell, Woodcock, Oxspring, Ridges, Cooper,
Hare
Scorers:- untraced

12. 04. 1898 Gravesend   (H)   1-1
Heath, Neil, Tranter, Barker, Oxspring,
Chisholm, Hird, Reid, Dove, Gresham, Woodcock
Scorer:- Woodcock

18. 04. 1898 Upton Park   (H)   3-0
Heath, Neil, Tranter, Barker, Oxspring,
Chisholm, Hird, Reid, Dove, Gresham, Woodcock
Scorers:- Hird 2, Woodcock

26. 04. 1898 Woolwich Arsenal   (H)   2-2
Heath, Neil, Tranter, Barker, Oxspring,
Chisholm, Hird, Reid, Dove, Gresham, Foss
Scorers:- Reid, Gresham

CHAPTER FIVE
TRAGEDY AND SUCCESS
1898/99

In the close season a tragedy happened at Thames Shipyard that was to affect a large number of families within the district. The launching of ships was not an unusual event, but on June 21st 1898 the 6,000 ton warship 'Albion' was due to be launched and this was to be the first 'Royal' launching at Thames Ironworks. The Duke and Duchess of York, who were later to become George V and Queen Mary, and other dignitaries arrived for the launching ceremony at 3. 00 pm, with the local crowd, who were mostly made up of women and children, excited at the thought of witnessing such distinguished people.

Around 30,000 spectators filled every available space, and with flags and bunting flying everywhere and with the perfect weather there was a carnival atmosphere. Most of the crowd were dressed in their Sunday best, probably the only other clothes that they possessed. The best vantage points for spectators were rapidly taken up, but there was a workmen's slipway alongside the uncompleted warship, the 'Shikishima' that gave an excellent view. This wooden gantry was not meant to hold large numbers of people and had been marked up with the sign 'Dangerous.' There were seventy policemen on duty, but with the benefit of hindsight, that number was insufficient. The policemen that were close to the gantry did clear it completely but as the launch time approached they appeared powerless to stop it filling again with 200 people.

As the dogshores supporting the 'Albion' were showing signs of collapsing it was decided to bring the launch forward ten minutes to 2.50 pm. The Duchess hurled the bottle of champagne at the hull but it did not break, nor did it do so with two further attempts, surely a traditional sign of bad luck. She had then to cut the cord signalling the workmen to release the dogshores. George Mackrow, the shipbuilding manager had thought that the 'Albion' would enter the water at a fair speed, but in doing so it caused a massive backlash of water like a tidal wave. The gantry caught the full force and snapped the wooden structure throwing all those upon it into the muddy waters of Bow Creek.

Due to the slipway's half hidden location others did not realise what had happened and their cheers for the launching blocked the screams of those struggling and drowning in the river. The Duke and Duchess, unaware of the situation, left with the other dignitaries and the remainder of the crowd made their way home. Those that were near to the tragic scene, spectators and workmen alike, desperately

The Albion nearly ready for launch

set about attempts to rescue those they could. Some of those thrown into the water were killed by the falling timbers and others were trampled on by other victims. Others just simply drowned. At first it was thought that not many had perished but a total of 38 was the final figure; many were saved by spectators diving into the water, with Thames Police pulling others from the river.

By early evening a temporary mortuary was set up in an engineering department shed after 24 bodies had been discovered. A galvanising shed was then quickly fitted out with wooden benches and an electrician, Fred Wilson by name, fitted lights to the building and the bodies were transferred there. Sadly, Fred discovered that his sister, who had recently been married, and his mother were amongst the dead. By 11.30 pm thirty-two bodies had been recovered. Their clothing was left in a bundle at their feet, for the relatives to identify their loved ones, and the corpses were covered with canvas.

Arnold Hills was totally shocked at the catastrophe and arranged to pay the bereaved families' funeral expenses and personally visited the families concerned. West Ham Council opened a disaster fund to help survivors as well as the bereaved, for most of the people involved were from desperately poor backgrounds.

The funerals were all carried out over the course of three days, the Saturday, Monday and Tuesday after the accident. Because of the criticism of the lack of police numbers at the tragedy there was a large number of officers in attendance at the cemetery over the three days in case of any trouble. The largest numbers of burials that took place were on the Saturday. Huge crowds lined the routes, many blinds were drawn, shopkeepers put up black shutters and flags flew at half-mast. On the Monday, the funeral included the five schoolchildren who were drowned in the disaster. Two of those were brother and sister, Ernest Hopkins aged 12 and Kittie aged 10. The children from the schools followed the carriages and most wore mourning and many wept. Perhaps the saddest story of all was the death of Mrs Isobel White aged 30 and her children Lottie 5, and Queenie 2. When Mrs White had been pulled from the water, rescuers had found her two little daughters still clinging to her frock.

Most of the funerals took place at the East London Cemetery. Some of the victims were interred individually but most were buried in a communal grave, which was subsequently marked by engraved tablets and a large anchor. Arnold Hills wrote later that when he visited the homes of the bereaved, he 'met with no shadow of bitterness, no tone of complaint. In some sense I represented the Company at whose doors the responsibility of this great accident lay; but none the less the mother weeping for her child, the husband heartbroken for the loss of his young wife, clasped my hand, and in broken accents told me how sorry they were that this terrible accident should have marred all the joyous festivities of the launch.'

Mr Hills may have been a considerate, sympathetic and compassionate man but as far as the bereaved were concerned, the meek acceptance of their lot after such a tragedy shows how attitudes today vastly differ to those of Victorian times.

At the inquest many questions were asked as to whether the wooden slipway should have been fenced off, or whether it was marked as dangerous, if enough police were employed to prevent spectators from gaining entry, or if the quality of the construction of the gantry could withstand the weight of a specified number of people. A large number of witnesses gave evidence, and it was pointed out that numerous launches had taken place at Blackwall without any such mishap having occurred. It had to be decided whether the deaths were accidental, or if there was culpable negligence or whether someone should be held responsible. After the Coroner had summed up the proceedings, the jury gave a verdict of 'accidental death', blaming a number of circumstances, i.e. visitors not obeying instructions to vacate the gantry, insufficient precautions which prevented people from doing so, and overcrowding which obstructed the police from being able to carry out their orders. They were also of the opinion that too many people were admitted to the launch and recommended that in future accommodation should be provided by specially erected stands.

As a tribute to the numerous acts of bravery that took place on that fateful day it is worth remembering just a few of the names of those that risked their own lives to save others. Tom Cook, aged 23 who came originally from Lowestoft and worked at the Ironworks saved 13 lives by repeatedly diving back into the river. Mr A. G. Colby of 47 Lawrence Street, Canning Town, pulled a total of thirteen people from the water. John Knock, 21 Blyth Street, Stratford saved seven people, and William Angus, a painter, who lived at 37 Whitethorne Street, Bow Common rescued eight.

After such a terrible tragedy a situation arose which could be described as either one of supreme irony or one of total disrespect. The Memorial Recreation Grounds were situated directly adjacent to the East London Cemetery and whilst the sombre funeral ceremonies were taking place on the Saturday, loud music from the band and the cheers of the spectators at Thames Ironworks' cycling event could clearly be heard.

It has been suggested that the disaster that occurred at the launching of the 'Albion' was still very much on Arnold Hills' mind and clouding his better judgement when he agreed to allow the football club to go fully professional in 1898/99. This may well have been the case but it is still difficult to understand why he took that decision. The new home venue at the Memorial Recreation Grounds, built at enormous cost as has been seen, had not created any substantial increase in the number of spectators coming in at the gate during the previous season, so introducing a fully professional outlook into the club would initially mean extra expenditure, which would only come from Hills' own pocket. The football committee, and Francis Payne in particular, must have used very persuasive arguments in favour, possibly urging Hills that by bringing professional players into the club, additional spectators would fill the ground and more than offset the extra outgoings. Bearing in mind Hills' views on the continuing participation of his own employees in the club rather than outsiders, and his public school background with his early involvement in strictly amateur sport, he must have agreed with a great deal of misgivings.

The real reasons will never be known, but whatever they were, the result was that professionalism was agreed upon, and entry into two leagues was applied for and accepted. The two leagues concerned were Division Two of the Southern League and the Thames & Medway Combination. Clubs were expected to field first-team players for both competitions. The latter league was the stronger of the two as it contained a higher grade of club, but the Ironworks committee agreed that they did not expect to have any ambitions of winning that particular title as they would be in the company of such clubs as New Brompton, Chatham, Gravesend and Tottenham Hotspur, all of whom were involved in the Southern League *First* Division.

It has been stated in other publications that of thirty players signed for the first team for 1898/99 there were just three players remaining from the previous campaign. This is well wide of the mark. There were twelve players retained and they were:- goalkeeper Heath, full backs Neil, Tranter and Rooff, half backs Chisholm, Dove and Barker, and forwards Hird, Gresham, James Reid, Foss and Woodcock. What is more, exactly half of that number featured in both competitions on a regular basis. The remaining 18 players were newcomers who were mainly professionals with a fair sprinkling of Scottish players amongst them. During the second half of the season, in a bid to strengthen the squad and give the team more options, they signed no less than eight full professionals who all played their part in, what turned out to be, a successful campaign.

The Ironworks played their first match of the season on September 1st 1898 on a Thursday evening at Sheppey United in a Thames & Medway Combination fixture, going down by the only goal in a disappointing display. Two days later on a very hot afternoon the first ever meeting between the Irons and 'Spurs took place at Northumberland Park in the same competition. It was so hot it was reported that *'A peculiar thing was noticed at Tottenham in the shape of specially improvised fans, which were being used for cooling purposes. It was absolutely necessary that something should be done to keep off the tropical heat, and in the near future we can see a fine opening......to invest in a supply of cheap fans.'*

This can only be described as bizarre. Where these fans were situated, how effectively they were powered and what benefit they provided can only be imagined. The report continued *'Thirst quenchers too, are essentials and were in great demand on Saturday, and the thermometer registered something like 90 degrees in the shade. Football under such conditions seems absurd, but the 4,500 spectators, who, as we say when it rains, 'braved the elements' saw a really decent game between the twenty two limp and sun-scorched players. The 'Spurs opponents were quite up to their reputed ability, and doubtless Thames Ironworks will be heard of to advantage later on, more especially as they are now fully fledged pro's, with heaps of money behind them up the ladder of football fame.'*

The latter remarks were a consistent theme after Thames had become a professional outfit. It appeared that everyone in football assumed the club had a never-ending supply of money. The financial reserves of Victorian Arnold Hills cannot be compared to the present-day billions of Roman Abramovich. As for the match, it ended in defeat. After going behind by one goal at the interval, the intense heat told its tale on the Irons, and 'Spurs ran out 3-0 winners. Two T & M Combination matches, two defeats. Not an auspicious start.

Worse was to come. The following Wednesday the Irons were 'on the road' yet again, this time against Kent side, New Brompton, in the same competition. Changes had to be made as Tommy Moore, Chisholm and Jimmy Reid were all injured. Rafter, the ex 3rd Grenadier Guards goalkeeper came in for Tommy but had to pick the ball out of the net four times in a 1-4 defeat.

Thames' first game in the Southern League Second Division came on the Saturday after their third T & M defeat and once again the team had to travel. Their opponents were Shepherds Bush (not to be confused with QPR). The home side had previously been known as Old St Stephen's but their committee thought that the name change would serve the interest of both club and the spectators, who were said to be delighted with the change as it was more relative to the area from where their support originated. The kick off was delayed until 4. 30 pm (reason unknown) and the attendance was 1,500. A 3-0 victory was obtained over the 'Bushmen', as they were to become known, with 20 year-old signing Atkinson grabbing two goals. This was the first of only two Southern League matches that the youngster would appear in, and with only 3 appearances in the T & M Combination, he did not play again. Thames did not have things all their own way as Moore was outstanding in goal prompting one observer to state that 'It didn't take long for the Directors of Millwall to realise that they had made a mistake in losing this player to the Ironworks. Why he was allowed to leave was a mystery as he never had a bad game, made very few mistakes, and proved himself a thoroughly reliable goalkeeper.'

The Thames committee's belief that the club had no likelihood of achieving success in the Thames & Medway Combination was confirmed when the club received a 2-5 drubbing at Gravesend a few days afterwards. The fixture arrangements did not exactly help, as this was the Irons' fourth consecutive away match in the Combination.

The Southern League provided the club with their first home game however, when on 24th September 1898 the 'old enemy' Brentford were the visitors. Once again it was a case of a team arriving late and the match began at 4.15 pm instead of 3. 30. In an exciting encounter the Irons were victorious by 3-1. Before the first goal was scored Gresham heavily charged the Brentford 'keeper as the ball was entering the net and the goal was quite rightly disallowed, but in the second half both Gresham and Hay bundled the goalkeeper into the net whilst he had the ball in his hands. The goal stood, for a goalkeeper could be charged with the ball in his hands, which was within the rules at the time and was for many years afterwards. Being the last line of defence in those days was not exactly the best position in the team.

The Irons began their F.A. Cup campaign the following week with a 2-0 victory over Royal Engineers Training Battalion with George Neil at centre half, making what was now to be a rare appearance in the first team.

The club finally played their first home match in the Thames & Medway Combination during the week after, but were nothing but consistent as they lost to Chatham 1-2, which made it five defeats from five games in this competition. The first victory did eventually come however, when Grays United were defeated 2-0 later in the month, but overall October turned out to be something of a disaster as Thames were knocked out of the F.A. Cup after Brighton United beat them in a replay at the Memorial Grounds and there were two consecutive defeats in the Southern League. Rather worrying was the fact that against Brighton in the Cup and Wycombe in the league four goals had been conceded in each match.

Remembering the awful events in June, when the 'Albion' tragedy occurred, there was stricter security in evidence at the shipyard when the Japanese battleship 'Shikishima' was successfully launched in November 1898. On this occasion Royalty was not present and instead of the usual bottle of champagne being thrust at the hull of the ship, a glass container of liquid perfume was used. This was not because Mr Arnold Hills considered that the previous attempts to break the bottle might have caused bad luck, but because of his utter contempt for alcohol in all its forms. Surely he would have preferred to see a bottle of champagne smashed rather than someone consume it?

Perhaps it was coincidental that the 'good luck' from the launch rubbed off on Thames Ironworks football club, as from this point on, it was definitely *not* a case of 'fortunes always hiding.' As far as the Thames & Medway Combination was concerned, the team suffered one defeat during November and then won eight of their final nine games, finishing in a respectable halfway position in the league against good class opposition.

The month of November was also successful for Thames in their Southern League campaign. One of the club's captures during the close season was David Lloyd who was an Army man serving in the 3rd Scots Guards, but who had played for Brentford during 1897/98. He was a big, strong player equally at home in defence or at centre forward. He began at the back, but by November was pushed up into attack and made an immediate impact scoring a hat-trick in an away match at St. Albans. With the ground shrouded in fog the game began late, but this did not prevent the local correspondent from being able to observe the action and proceeding to give a not exactly unbiased account. He began :- '...*the referee would not have exceeded his duty if he had sent McEwan* (Thames) *off, for every time he was beaten he deliberately tripped players up, although they were outside the 12 yards. Watkins* (St. Albans) *however, was not so fortunate, for he fouled a man and the referee gave a penalty, severe punishment in the circumstances, bearing in mind the punishment he had received.'* In the second half the fog partially lifted, but because of the late start it was practically twilight and not much could be seen, which was just as well as far as the local reporter was concerned, as the Irons ran out 4-1 winners.

The first game in December saw the start of the club's remarkable match winning run of 15 consecutive victories to the end of the season. They opened the month with a home fixture against Fulham, winning by 2-1. Considering the latter day West Ham United's reputation for playing football in the right manner and style (and very often over-doing it) it is interesting to read a report of the club's predecessors usual pattern of play.

The correspondent of 'The Chelsea Mail' conceded that *'On the play the Irons were a much cleverer and smarter team. The forwards excelled in tricky work but against a determined defence like the Reds I think it was overdone......there was a vast difference in the styles of the two lines of forwards, the Reds adopting the kick and rush plan and the Irons the quick, short passing method.* He then went on to praise the Thames full backs:- *'...the Irons backs were as safe as the Bank. I cannot call to mind a single instance when either Margeram or Tranter miskicked and their judgement was great. The Reds forwards had a job to pass this pair...'*

Sadly, passions ran high on the terraces, for when McEachrane scored and the goal was ruled offside *'...this displeased the crowd and before the free-kick was taken Mr Heard* (the referee) *informed a section of the spectators that unless their remarks were less personal they would be removed...'*

When Watford were defeated by 2-1 at the Memorial Grounds Lloyd was in evidence again scoring both goals. His first came when the opposing 'keeper could not hold his initial shot and he netted from the rebound, and the second came when he headed in a 'beauty'. Thames should have added more but were continually caught offside. They could not add to their score although, as someone remarked 'golden chances were as plentiful as blackberries in September.'

A 3-0 victory at Chesham on Christmas Eve was followed by another away match at Maidenhead on New Year's Eve. When Tommy Moore missed his train and was unable to get the game the irrepressible Charlie Dove showed his versatility by taking over in goal and not conceding in a 4-0 win. The score would have been even greater had it not been for the heroics of Dove's opposite number in Maidenhead's goal, who on one occasion saved three rapid shots in succession. An odd situation occurred before the match when two official referees put in an appearance. Due to an error at HQ one should have been officiating at the Fulham v Watford fixture!

As the New Year of 1899 hove into view it is worth remembering that those families in the area of South West Ham, in addition to the employees at Thames Ironworks & Shipbuilding Company, lived in a locality that depended on its existence chiefly by commerce, and very much relied on work that revolved around maritime affairs. On the whole 1898 had seen a number of distressing events. As well as the 'Albion' disaster, an explosion aboard the 'Manitoba' moored in the Albert Dock resulted in the death of five workmen. This was followed by news that the 7,000 ton liner 'Mohegan' had foundered in a mysterious manner off the Cornish coast in the Falmouth Bay area. No less than 34 West Ham members of the crew, many of them heads of families, found a watery grave. Such tragedies were not forgotten but every month there were also individual fatal accidents in the docks and in ship's holds. On the bright side, the launching of the 'Shikishima' had been a success, a Lifeboat Saturday Fund had been established and on a more cultural theme, the Thames Ironworks Band had won the local band contest.

Unfortunately as far as the footballing side of Thames Ironworks was concerned, despite the team producing good entertainment and winning matches, attendances at the Memorial Grounds were very disappointing. The secretary's view had already been expressed in the Thames Ironworks Gazette, '*I regret to say that from a financial point of view it has been a hard struggle. We are very much indebted to the kindness of our President* (Mr Arnold Hills), *who from time to time has assisted us in paying our debts, but it is very discouraging to us to feel that we have little or no support from the Works, and that among the very admirers of football that live in the neighbourhood of Canning Town, so few attend our matches.*'

This was the case when the Irons entertained Wycombe Wanderers on January 14th 1899. On the back of an unbeaten run of seven matches, and with the acquisition of the very experienced Tommy Dunn from Wolves, together with Pat Leonard from Manchester City who had scored a hat-trick on his debut in a friendly match, a miserly attendance of 1,000 spectators came through the gates. They could not have complained at the fare provided. Mirroring the Irons' predicament when they arrived without a goalkeeper at Maidenhead, Wycombe did likewise. Turner, their full-back, went between the sticks, but unlike the Irons they had no twelfth man to fall back on, so one of their followers pulled on a shirt to complete the team! Thames gained ample revenge for their earlier season defeat, running out 4-1 winners, with Lloyd bagging another brace, although the visitors gave a good account of themselves with Moore having to 'make three saves with his hands'. Once again however, it was reported that '*a certain section of the crowd, happily very small, made some very objectionable remarks to the Wycombe players. It is to be hoped that these enthusiast's behaviour will not be repeated.*' At least it could be said that the club did have dedicated support of some kind.

Perhaps the greatest danger to the Ironworks losing their winning streak came the following week when they visited Wolverton. The home side were the Irons closest rivals and eventually finished as runners-up scoring 88 goals in the process! In contrast to the fog earlier in the season the match was played in weather that was described as a hurricane, in front of a crowd of just 200 hardy souls. The home side, with the benefit of the gale blowing behind them, rushed to a three-goal lead by half-time, but in the second half the tables were turned. Leonard led the fight back with a goal from a corner 15 minutes after the break, then scored another shortly afterwards. The third came from a wind assisted long shot from Chisholm to bring the scores level. Moore in goal, played his part by saving a penalty, before all the points were secured by Thames with Dove's goal in the last few minutes.

The month of January was seen out by the club's biggest victory to date when Chesham were the unlucky recipients of an 8-1 drubbing. It was an excellent performance all round but it also highlighted the maverick peculiarities of Tommy Moore in goal. He was becoming well known for his eccentric forays outside of the area, but this game was so one-sided that during the second half he spent the greater part of it upfield. He was caught out however, right at the end of the match when the Chesham left winger broke away on his own and put the ball into the empty net without a Thames defender to be seen. Already eight goals to the good, it was of no consequence except to the embarrassment of Tommy.

It does seem amazing, but until 1912 goalkeepers were allowed to handle, but not carry, the ball anywhere in their own half of the field, which meant that in theory they could knock it up to the halfway line with their hands to help an attack! This would take some bravery, not to say skill to achieve, and something for the referee to keep his eyes on, because goalkeepers at this time wore the same jerseys as their team-mates, not the distinctive outfits that are worn today.

In late January the Warmley club from Bristol disbanded and the Thames secretary, Francis Payne, showed his initiative by signing three of their players. They were George Reid who was originally with Reading at the same time as the current

Irons forward James Reid (no relation), Henderson, a free-scoring forward, and Peter McManus the ex-West Bromwich Albion and Edinburgh St Bernards defender, who was serving a two-week suspension at the time. All played their part in both the Southern League Second Division and Thames & Medway Combination remaining fixtures.

(Warmley were one of two clubs that were situated in the Bristol East area, the other being Bristol St George. As both clubs were on the verge of collapse at the same time it was believed that one successful club could be raised from an amalgamation, but it was said that the two sets of supporters and officials hated one another so much that this was not considered an advisable option! Things do not change and it is possible to think of a number of clubs that would feel the same way today).

Unfortunately the wages of those professional players engaged at the shipyard is not known, but in February Arnold Hills, the Managing Director, gave his annual speech to employees and their relatives. His creation of the Good Fellowship Scheme, which made possible his successful experiment of the Eight Hour Day system where each man was awarded according to his work and subsequently received a profit dividend, had clearly demonstrated advantages both to the employer and employee. The wage bill had risen by 143 percent, but the increase in output was considerable. It was Hills' belief that the interests of Capital and Labour were one and the same, and he was convinced that the secret of success was to be found in co-operation between the two. Unfortunately, during the first decade of the new century, Hills found that he could not compete with the lower prices of the Northern shipyards and contracts were lost which led to the eventual demise of the company.

Relatively good wages however, still did not give rise to any greater increase in spectator numbers at the Memorial Grounds. A 2-0 triumph at Brentford, which meant eight consecutive victories in the Southern League, drew a paltry 1,500 attendance when Uxbridge were the visitors. This was a pity because those that were absent missed new boy Henderson score all four goals in a 4-0 success. This was the first time that a player had scored as many in a competitive match for the Irons, but what made it more impressive was that all the goals came in the first twenty-six minutes.

Without a first team fixture at the end of February the Ironworks arranged a friendly visit to Eastbourne FC. During the 1890s and the early part of the 20th Century the Sussex club regarded themselves as 'minor Corinthians', playing only cup-ties and friendly matches. They paid professional clubs a fee to travel to the Saffrons Ground for challenge matches, raising the price of admission from 6d to one shilling to cover the cost of their guarantee.

The local correspondent was full of praise for Thames, declaring that '...the visitors made a most honourable impression on the crowd......by their play, which, apart from its cleverness, was of such a strictly fair and gentlemanly character as to put many an amateur team to the blush. Their footwork was a treat to watch and their accurate heading was a feature of the game.' The team's outfit had been remarked upon several times during the season, with the colours becoming closer to the eventual claret and blue of West Ham United. Our Eastbourne friend went into overdrive 'A prettier and more distinctive costume than theirs I have never yet seen on a football ground. Light blue shirts, white knickers and scarlet stockings were their colours...their visit was highly appreciated by every one of the thousand-odd spectators who saw them.' Pure flattery! For the record the Irons won 3-1 with Leonard scoring twice.

The month of March saw the club continuing its winning run. Southall were disposed of away from home by 2-0 with Henderson grabbing both goals, with a crowd of 4,000 watching on. McManus made his debut at centre half in the 1-0 victory over St Albans and it was stated that *'(he) played a clever game and his clean methods afforded a striking contrast to the foul play of his opposite number.'*

During the midweek following, the Irons gained their first ever success against 'Spurs in any competition in a 2-1 win in the Thames & Medway Combination, but with eleven straight wins in the Southern League, attendances were still disappointing so the Thames committee arranged for horse-drawn buses to run from Canning Town station to the Memorial Grounds in an attempt to increase the gate, but only one thousand turned up to see Wolverton defeated by 2-1. However, by the following Saturday when Thames had the return fixture with Southall, word must have spread regarding the extra transport arrangements, as 3,000 spectators came through the gate, which was the biggest attendance of the season at home so far. Perhaps they were also satisfied with the entertainment and the result as the Irons notched up their thirteenth consecutive victory with a 2-0 win.

The Ironworks' final away fixture entailed a visit to Fulham at Craven Cottage, a match that was eagerly awaited by the West London club. Since the last meeting between the two teams, when the Irons winning run began, the Fulham club had turned professional themselves and it was expected that the home side would provide stiff opposition. When the teams appeared on the ground for the appointed kick-off time, the referee was nowhere to be seen, so the players had to 'warm up' for a full fifteen minutes until he arrived.

Fulham began the match on the attack, but Tranter was in fine form heading one shot round for a corner and then blocking another. After the early scares Thames were continually on the attack, 'beautifully backed up by their halves'. Maile, the home keeper, saved brilliantly until five minutes before the break, when he could not hold a hard shot and Lloyd (who was to join Fulham the following season) popped in the rebound. With the wind behind them in the second half Fulham pressed for a while but Moore stood firm and the Irons eventually came away with another victory.

Another attendance of 3,000 at the Memorial Grounds witnessed the last game of the campaign when Maidenhead were the visitors. This was just too easy for the Irons as Maidenhead turned up with only ten men. This was something that they had done on several occasions at away fixtures, and they were slaughtered to the tune of 10-0 with Lloyd scoring his second hat-trick of the season and Leonard bagging four.

The Ironworks were worthy winners of the Southern League Division Two by a margin of ten points, but Cowes from the Isle of Wight had won all their ten matches in the South West Section of Division Two, which meant a play-off to decide which club would take the title. Despite having to play this important game the Irons fielded exactly the same eleven players just two days before in the last, and unimportant, Thames & Medway Combination League match against Sheppey United. It is both surprising and admirable that throughout a 3-2 victory the team put as much effort into the game as they were to do against Cowes: something that most modern day players would be unlikely to do considering the circumstances.

The play-off itself was scheduled to be played at East Ferry Road, home of Millwall. The Cowes club were understandably infuriated at this choice of venue, as it meant a day trip for them whereas the Ironworks had just three miles to travel, but no change was made and the game went ahead. Early in the match Tranter appeared to deliberately handle the ball in the area, but the referee failed to notice. Cowes' play was characterised by their insistence in kicking long and high against the Irons defence which was far too strong to be caught out. Lloyd scored after 15 minutes, despite being tackled by both full backs but Jimmy Reid wrenched his knee ten minutes before the break and in that time Cowes surprisingly equalised when Moore let the ball drop over his head and into the net. In the second half Reid returned and Henderson put Thames in front again inside three minutes, and after a couple of scares Leonard put the outcome beyond doubt with the third goal, giving the Ironworks the title.

Winning the title did not bring automatic promotion however, as Thames Ironworks and Cowes from the Second Division had to play Test Matches against the bottom two clubs respectively in the First Division, Sheppey United and R.A. Portsmouth, to decide who would eventually appear in the top division.

The Irons were obliged to be the travellers on this occasion, meeting Sheppey United at neutral Chatham, but once more the train did not 'take the strain' as both the Ironworks team and the referee arrived over an hour late after a derailment, fortunately without any injuries to passengers. There was not much sympathy from the local correspondent however, with his pre-match comments. It was not the first, nor would it be the last time that the Thames club would be criticized for having financial backing. *'The Ironworks executive'* he began *'has made especial efforts to obtain admission into the First Division of the Southern League next year and they are admitted to be a greatly improved team. The 'Hills Boy' places plenty of capital at their back with the probability of acquiring an exceptionally strong team for next season; it stands to reason that all the trouble and expense was not made without aiming at transference into the elite of Southern League circles. They made no attempt to conceal their aspirations, and a general consensus of opinion posted them out as likely to be one of the admitted teams, whether they won the test match or not.'* (There had been rumours prior to the test matches that the Southern League were looking to increase the number of clubs in the First Division for 1899/1900.)

During the hour or so prior to the eventual kick off there had been heavy rain, which had then ceased, but a strong wind marred the game, although Sheppey won the toss and had the wind advantage, which meant heavy pressure on the Irons' defence. The Kent side were cheered on by the Chatham crowd as well as their own supporters and drew first blood, scoring from the boot of Collins. They were on top for a while, but because of 'dallying' on the ball lost their advantage, and Thames equalised just after half-time through Lloyd. Play was even after this and extra time was required, but there was no further score. The local correspondent declared *'with the Londoners deliberately kicking the ball out of the ground......and thereby achieving their object.'*

Before a replay could take place, the Southern League management committee decided to expand the First Division for the following season and accepted all four Test Match contestants together with QPR and Bristol Rovers.

So ended the Irons' first professional campaign. The close season, although being a busy one for the club, was also to see the downfall of Francis Payne and his involvement as secretary with Thames Ironworks FC.

PEN PICTURES

Charles Dove *born Millwall, June Qtr 1877*

Charlie was the only player to play in each of the five complete seasons of Thames Ironworks FC. He had special footballing talents from his days as a schoolboy, and was a regular and captain of Park School, West Ham. In a school article written two years after he had left, he was remembered as being without comparison to the current crop of youngsters. He turned out for Forest Swifts Juniors and as a 15 year old played for local side Plaistow Melville in 1892/93. He also made appearances for South West Ham, but whilst he was employed as an apprentice at Thames Ironworks the Company team was formed, and he became a regular in the side making at least 18 appearances and scoring 6 known goals in that first season, but due to a number of unrecorded statistics it was certainly many more. He could play with equal skill in any position on the field, which he did over the course of his career, even to the extent of playing in goal in a Southern League Division Two match against Maidenhead when he deputised for Tommy Moore, being unbeaten in a 4-0 victory. When the Irons joined the London League in their second season he missed just one game and played in all eight London Senior Cup matches. He also made a total of eleven overall appearances in the Essex Senior Cup, West Ham Charity Cup and friendlies. His season's total goal tally was 9.

Standing at 5ft 11in tall and weighing twelve stone he was not only a very skilful all-round player, but he was absolutely fearless. Due to this commitment in his play he sustained a number of injuries, one of which came after a collision with Arthur Oxspring (later to become a team-mate) in a friendly game against local rivals South West Ham on Christmas Day 1897, which put him out of action until April 1898. Maybe, due to his enthusiasm, he returned too soon, for in the vital London League championship match against the 2nd Grenadier Guards he was badly kicked early on in the first half and had to leave the field for the rest of the match. Charlie was in the thick of it again the following season when in a Thames & Medway Combination fixture in November 1898, he 'came into collision' with a Chatham opponent causing an on-field fracas.

He was nothing if not 100% committed. Almost exactly a year later he received a dislocated jaw after 'banging heads' with a New Brompton forward, but gutsy as ever, he was back two weeks later playing in a vital F.A. Cup match against Millwall. In March 1900, due to injuries received, he was advised by his doctor to call it a day, but the advice was ignored and Charlie was to take part in Thames Ironworks evolvement into West Ham United in 1900/01. He was a regular in the first half of the season, but after an ankle injury at Portsmouth, he was no longer considered on a frequent basis and in 1901/02 he joined local rivals Millwall, but his injuries caught up with him and he retired from football in 1902/03.

For Thames Ironworks he played at least 120 first team matches, which does not include a number of appearances in friendly matches in Thames last two seasons; a remarkable figure for an amateur player. When the club became West Ham United he notched up a further 16.

He worked at the shipbuilding yard, rising from an apprentice to the rank of shipwright, following in the industry in the footsteps of his father George, who had been a ships carpenter. Charlie was another player who remained an amateur and was living at that time at 97 Selsdon Road, West Ham.

Tommy Dunn *born Falkirk, June 2nd 1873 Died June 24th 1938*

Began his career at Wolverhampton Wanderers in 1891/92 where he gave strong, consistent performances at full-back, making 88  appearances for the First Division side, and gaining an F.A. Cup runners-up medal with them in 1895/96. During the following campaign he joined fellow First Division side Burnley making six appearances, but made just one more in 1897/98 before joining Kent side Chatham in the Southern League, turning out for them on seven occasions in 1898/99 before moving to Thames Ironworks later that season and assisting them in their Southern League 2nd Division Championship title win, playing in 13 matches including a Championship decider and a Test Match. He also turned out 4 times in the Thames & Medway Combination. He was a regular in the club's final season making 22 appearances in the Southern League (including one Test Match) seven in the F.A. Cup, and seven in the Thames & Medway Combination. He never lost his strong Scottish brogue and eventually returned to Scotland where he took up an undertakers business.

George Gresham *born Gainsborough 1874*

Came down from Lincolnshire after playing for Gainsborough Trinity who were in the Midland League at the time. George was one of the early pioneers of the Thames Ironworks club and in the initial season of 1895/96 played at least 22 times for them, scoring on 10 occasions. Apart from laying on chances for team mates, he was better

known as a goalscoring inside forward, having the knack of always making himself available to his colleagues. He was on the small side at 5ft 6in but quite speedy and enthusiastic, which often resulted in him getting caught offside, a law which at that time required *three* of the opposition to be between the player making his forward pass and the goal-line, and as a consequence a number of his goals were disallowed. He played a prominent part in four of the five seasons of the Ironwork's existence, and gained medals for their London League Championship in 1897/98, in which he did not miss one game, and the Southern League Second Division Championship the following season when he played in the majority of fixtures. He also gained representative honours when he was chosen to represent Essex against Norfolk in October 1897. He finished with a total known record of 110 first team appearances with 48 goals scored, which proves what a valuable asset he was to the team. He always remained an amateur and was employed at the yard as a ships plater.

R. Henderson

Played for Southern League First Division side Warmley (Bristol) in 1898/99 scoring nine goals in fifteen appearances. When the club folded in February 1899 Thames snapped him up and he proved a valuable acquisition to the forward line. In both league competitions he scored a combined total of 10 goals in fifteen appearances and became the first Ironworks player to score four goals in a competitive match, all of which came in the first 26 minutes of a Southern League Second Division match against Uxbridge. He represented the Southern League against London F A, and gained further representative honours appearing for the Thames & Medway Combination, scoring twice against the United League in March 1899. After a short half season with the Irons he left the club and joined Gravesend United for 1899/1900. With such an aptitude for scoring, and with his representative record, it was surprising that the Kent club arranged a special friendly match against the Royal Lancashire Fusiliers in order to establish his ability. Impressed by his performance when he promptly scored 4 goals in the match, he was given a first team place and he scored a creditable 11 goals in 20 appearances. He made only 4 appearances the following season without scoring before this rather shadowy figure, about whom

very little else is known, disappeared from the senior game altogether.

Henry Hird *born West Hartlepool, Sept Qtr 1874*

Came down from Stockton on Tees early in the 1897/98 season. Was specifically an 'out and out' right winger, but did occasionally play as a wing half. Although reasonably tall at 5ft 10in he was a very fast and tricky winger, whose crosses were of a high quality, so much so that a number of goals came as a result of his accuracy during the season that the Irons won the London League Championship. He was also capable of scoring himself, occasionally preferring to have a shot at goal rather than cross the ball, and netted 5 goals in the league and four in friendly matches. He was a regular in 1898/99 making 19 appearances and scoring 3 goals when the Irons won the Southern League Second Division Championship, but he laid on many goals for others. He also made 12 starts in the Thames & Medway Combination, scoring on 3 occasions, and 3 in the F.A. Cup scoring one goal. One game that he started but did not finish was a London League match against Leyton in October 1897 when he got his marching orders, which made him the first (known) Irons player to be dismissed. Henry made just one Southern League, one T & M and three F.A. Cup appearances in 1899/1900, but continued in his employment at the yard as a ships plater, living at 33 St Martins Avenue, East Ham

Alf Hitch *born Walsall, March Qtr 1877*

Began his career with local amateur side Walsall Unity before joining Walsall FC in 1897, who were then members of the Football League Second Division. He played just two games for them before coming south to Thames Ironworks one year later. He appeared in three Southern League Division Two, one Thames & Medway, and two F.A. Cup matches in the number 5 shirt before moving across London to QPR for their initial campaign in the Southern League First Division. In two seasons he made 49 appearances and scored 5 goals, and his outstanding half back play was recognised when he was chosen to play in an England trial (South v North) in February 1901. This brought him to the attention of First Division Nottingham Forest who signed him for 1901/02. He married a girl from the local area in December 1901, but after only 13 games he returned to QPR the following season. He re-established himself there staying for four seasons, making 118 appearances and scoring 14 goals. He last club was Watford, also a Southern League club. Signing for them in 1906/07, he was a regular for two seasons playing 60 games for them, scoring just once. He had a very colourful life after his footballing career, becoming a gold prospector, and circus promoter in Australia and in the 1920s was one of the early pioneers in the promotion of speedway 'Down Under'.

Patrick Leonard *born Scotland 1877*

Patrick was a winger who also had an eye for goal, and it was a pity that over four seasons in senior football he played so few games. His career began at St Mirren in the Scottish league in 1896/97 where he scored two goals in ten appearances. He attracted the attention of Manchester City then in the Football League Second Division, appearing in fifteen league matches and scoring four goals. He came down to Kent to join New Brompton the following season but only made one first team appearance before Thames Ironworks signed him in January 1899. He promptly scored a hat-trick in a friendly match against Upton Park and netted seven goals in ten matches in the Southern League Championship winning side, and also scored in the Championship decider. For the 1899/1900 campaign he re-joined Manchester City, but made only one appearance, scoring in an early season 4-0 victory, but was released the following summer.

David Lloyd *born Hackney, June Qtr 1872*

David was an Army man pursuing his career in the 3rd Grenadier Guards, when he became a member of their football club in 1896/97. He won the first of his four footballing medals that season when the Guards won the London League Championship. He was a strong, powerful player 6ft tall and weighing in at 13st 2lbs, being equally comfortable in defence or attack. He was dominant in the air in any position and scored many goals with his head. He joined Brentford in his second season and won a London Senior Cup medal with them before switching to Thames

Ironworks in 1898/99. He began at the heart of the defence but by November 1898 he was pushed up into the forward line to good effect in both the Southern League Division Two and Thames & Medway Combination. He scored an amazing 14 goals in 13 appearances in the former and 6 goals in 11 in the latter. With the Irons lifting the Southern League Division Two title David had acquired 3 medals in three seasons, but he then joined Fulham in 1899 and in two seasons scored 24 goals in 43 matches in all competitions.

His army career then took priority when he was called to the Guards colours for active service in the Boer War in South Africa. He returned to Fulham in 1902/03 and proved his versatility by moving back into the defence, but even in that position he scored 12 goals in 31 competitive competitions helping Fulham to win the Southern League Division Two title and giving him the last of his four medals, all with four different clubs. The following campaign Fulham filled their side with professionals and David played just 3 games, all in the F.A. Cup, scoring 2 goals. He signed for amateur club Willesden Town in August 1904. As a postscript he played one Southern League match for Fulham in goal in 1901, just as Charlie Dove had done for the Irons two years earlier, strangely enough against the same club, Maidenhead United.

Roderick McEachrane *born Inverness Scotland, February 3rd 1877 Died 1952*

Came down from Scotland in 1898 to work in the shipbuilding yard and play for Thames Ironworks. Roddy, as he was popularly known, became a constructive, but hard tackling wing-half. The duties of a half back in those days were mainly of a defensive nature with the responsibility of backing up the forwards when it was deemed necessary. Although Roddy was generally a quiet man, both on and off the field, it was said that he kept his team-mates in good humour with his ready wit. He also possessed an 'iron will' which was demonstrated in an early season home match against Southampton at the Memorial Grounds in West Ham United's first season of 1900/01, when a large mob invaded the pitch during half-time and Roddy used his powers of persuasion to move them back onto the terraces. In his time with the Ironworks he totted up 53 Southern League and 10 F.A. Cup appearances, and missed just one out of 26 Thames & Medway Combination matches, and when the club evolved into West Ham United he made another 53 appearances in the Southern League and 7 in the F.A. Cup. His consistently fine displays saw Woolwich Arsenal coming in for him and he joined them in 1902/03. He became a big favourite at Plumstead notching up an amazing 313 Football League appearances up to and including 1913/14 when the club had their first season at Highbury.

Peter McManus *born Wynchburgh Scotland, 1873*

Peter was a half-back who played mainly in the centre of the line. He made the first team at the Edinburgh club known as St. Bernards Athletic where he made 15 Scottish league appearances and won a Scottish Cup winners medal in 1894/95, but made only one Scottish Cup appearance the following campaign. He then came South in 1896, and played for First Division West Bromwich Albion for two seasons making 28 appearances and scoring one goal. He joined the Bristol club, Warmley, of the Southern League for 1898/99 and had made 12 starts for them before they disbanded and resigned from the league in January 1899. He was one of three players picked up immediately from the defunct club by Thames Ironworks. At 5ft 7ins and 12st he was a stocky and well-built player, strong in the tackle, gutsy and hard working, and said to 'take any amount of knocking about', although he was serving a two week suspension when he signed. He made 5 appearances in the Irons Southern League Two side that eventually won their league and appeared in the end of season Test match. In addition he played in 4 Thames & Medway Combination matches. His final season of 1899/1900 saw him appear in 5 Southern league Division One games, 4 in the F.A. Cup (1goal), and three in the T & M Combination.

Tommy Moore *born Stoke, 1877*

Began his senior career at Southern League First Division side Millwall in 1896/97 playing on 21 occasions over two seasons. Joined Thames Ironworks at the start of their Southern League Division Two campaign in 1898/99. Over the following two seasons he put in many outstanding performances. He was relatively short for a goalkeeper standing at something over 5ft 8ins but what he lacked in height he made up for in keen perception. He possessed good judgment and was as agile as a cat. He did on occasions however, have a rush of blood and race well out beyond the confines of his penalty area, and it seems as if the phrase 'between the sticks' didn't always apply to him. Indeed, up to 1912 goalkeepers were allowed to handle (but not carry) the ball in their own half which seems astonishing now.

Playing well out of goal, at certain times, does not appear to have been all that rare, for in an interview with Hugh Montieth, who was Tommy's successor in goal, the point was made that Hugh was one of the 'stay at home' goalkeepers. 'I don't believe in touring up among the half backs,' he said 'They can mind their own game, and I like them to let me mind mine.' In those days, of course, goalkeepers were not protected like they are today and numerous goals were scored when 'keepers, even whilst holding the ball were bundled over the line for a legitimate goal. On the other hand, when the penalty kick was introduced in 1891, and until goal area markings were altered just over ten years later, goalkeepers were allowed the freedom to advance 6 yards off their line when a penalty kick was taken. In a match report of game against New Brompton in 1899 it was stated that 'when the penalty kick was taken the ball went straight to Moore, *who had come out to his six yard line.*' On another occasion, with Moore coming out to the same distance, the penalty taker struck the ball against the bar. Obviously, when the law was altered and the 'keeper had to stay on his line the penalty taker's chances of scoring were greatly increased. Tommy was the regular first team choice for the Irons final two seasons making 51 Southern League appearances (including deciders and test matches), 10 F.A. Cup games and 21 Thames & Medway Combination matches. When Thames Ironworks became West Ham United he played just four matches due to the signing of the experienced Hugh Montieth, who had played for Celtic, Loughborough Town and Bristol City and would go on to gain an F.A. Cup winners medal in 1903 with Bury.

Tommy had his revenge after signing for Grays the following season. They were drawn to face West Ham United in the F.A. Cup and Moore put on a magnificent display helping the village side to an unexpected 2-1 victory at the Memorial Grounds: the first of a number of humiliating defeats in years to come against lower opposition in the F.A. Cup.

George Neil *born Poplar, December Qtr 1874*
Died 1905

George's first club was Millwall in 1891/92, where he spent three seasons, almost all in the reserves. This was followed by three seasons at West Norwood, two of which were as captain. Standing at just under 5ft 11in and at 12 stone he was a very accomplished full back, who could play on either flank, and when asked in an interview when his career was over, what he thought his strengths were, he replied 'Well, I don't think it was kicking or tackling; I should say it was coolness more than anything'. He first assisted the Ironworks as a guest player in a memorable friendly match against First Division West Bromwich Albion under electric light at Hermit Road in March 1896, and again that season against local side St Luke's on Good Friday 1896.

The following season in the first round of the London Senior Cup in October, George played his captain's role for West Norwood against the Irons when the Canning Town lads won through to the next round. According to a press report George was 'worthy of special mention'. Strangely enough he was allowed to play *for* the Ironworks the following week in a London League match against Crouch End, but did not play again for the club until 1897/98 when he joined them on a permanent basis. He missed only two of 16 London League matches in a campaign that saw the Irons win that Championship. He also played twice in the London Senior Cup and in at least eight friendly matches. He appeared in just two games in 1898/99 and then took over as Secretary when Francis Payne resigned. He made an immediate impact when, in the close season, he signed three very experienced and polished players from 'Spurs in Billy Joyce, Kenny McKay and Harry Bradshaw. Initially Arnold Hills steadfastly refused to agree to the transfers due to the cost involved, but George must have used very persuasive arguments in favour, and the deals were done. Syd King, later to become Manager took over as Secretary in 1902, and sadly, George died at the age of thirty in early 1905.

George Reid *born Blackland Mill*

Geordie, as he was known, scored 13 goals in 30 matches over two seasons from 1895/96 for Southern League side Reading. He had a successful goalscoring partnership with namesake James Reid over that period and they were later to play together in several matches for the Ironworks. After Reading, Geordie moved on to the Bristol club Warmley who were to

unfortunately fold in February 1899, but he was snapped up by Thames Ironworks along with Peter McManus and R. Henderson. He played in six matches, scoring once, towards the end of their Southern League Second Division championship campaign, and made just two appearances in the Thames & Medway Combination before he left and went back to his native Scotland, where he played for St Mirren.

In 1905/06 he was picked up by First Division side Middlesbrough and scored 5 goals in 24 appearances, but he returned to Scotland once again the following season and played for Johnstone. Bradford Park Avenue, surprisingly playing in the Southern League in 1907/08, brought Geordie back to England, and he was their top scorer with 12 goals from 33 appearances, but when they were accepted into the Football League Second Division for the following campaign he did not score in five outings and came further south to play for Brentford in the same season. The West London club gave him the most successful spell of his career as he was top scorer there for three seasons. In his last full season he scored 21 goals in 34 appearances, exactly half the club's total. He managed just 4 starts in his last season there, but still found the net 3 times. He could not resist the lure of Scotland however, and he went back to end his career with Clyde during the same season of 1911/12, his ninth club spanning 17 seasons.

J. Reynolds

Came from Southern League Gravesend United where he played for two seasons from 1896/97. He made 15 appearances scoring 6 times in that period. Joining Thames Ironworks in 1898/99, he was renowned for his 'screw shots' and the ability to bend free-kicks. He was essentially an out and out right-winger, but did, on several occasions fill other forward positions. Appearing on the left flank in one game, he came in for some criticism from the football correspondent of a local journal when it was stated that *'The outside left was notably weak, and if the management intend playing Reynolds in that position, I would advise supplying him with two 'right' boots. He can do nothing with the left.'* He must have had a bad day on that occasion because Reynolds was never on the losing side during the club's Southern League Second Division Championship campaign, making 15 appearances and scoring 5 goals. He also played in six Thames & Medway Combination matches, scoring once, but left at the end of the season.

Southern League Div Two 1898/99

10. 09. 1898 Shepherds Bush (A) 3-0
1500
Moore, Tranter, Margeram, Chisholm, Dove, McEachrane, Hird, Brett, Atkinson, Adams, Foss
Scorers:- Atkinson 2, Adams

24. 09. 1898 Brentford (H) 3-1
1200
Moore, Tranter, Lloyd, Chisholm, Hitch, McEachrane, Hird, Hay, Atkinson, Gresham, Dove
Scorers:- Hay 2, Dove

08. 10. 1898 Uxbridge (A) 1-2
2000
Moore, Lloyd, Dove, Chisholm, Hitch, McEachrane, Hird, Hay, Adams, Gresham, Cobb
Scorer:- Gresham

29. 10. 1898 Wycombe (A) 1-4
1000
Moore, Tranter, Dove, Chisholm, Hitch, McEachrane, Hird, J Reid, Hay, Gresham, Buller
Scorer:- Reid

05. 11. 1898 Shepherds Bush (H) 1-0
1000
Moore, Tranter, Margeram, Dove, McEwan, McEachrane, Reynolds, J Reid, Wenham, Gresham, Cobb
Scorer:- Wenham

12. 11. 1898 St. Albans (A) 4-1
800
Moore, Tranter, Margeram, Neil, McEwan, Chisholm, Hird, J Reid, Lloyd, Gresham, McEachrane
Scorers:- Lloyd 3, Reid

26. 11. 1898 Watford (A) 0-0
1000
Moore, Tranter, Margeram, Chisholm, McEwan, McEachrane, Hird, J. Reid, Hay, Gresham, Reynolds

03. 12. 1898 Fulham (H) 2-1
2000
Moore, Tranter, Margeram, Dove, McEwan, Chisholm, Hird, Reynolds, Hay, Gresham, McEachrane
Scorers:- Reynolds, Gresham

17. 12. 1898 Watford (H) 2-1
1500
Moore, Tranter, Margeram, Chisholm, McEwan, Hay, Reynolds, Hird, Lloyd, Gresham, McEachrane
Scorers:- Lloyd 2

24. 12. 1898 Chesham (A) 3-0
1000
Moore, Tranter, Margeram, Dove, McEwan, McEachrane, Hird, Reynolds, Lloyd, Hounsell, Gresham
Scorers:- Hird 2, Hounsell

31. 12. 1898 Maidenhead (A) 4-0
2000
Dove, Margeram, Neil, McEwan, Hird, McEachrane, Reynolds, Hounsell, Lloyd, J. Reid, Gresham
Scorers:- McEwan, Hird, Reynolds, Reid

14. 01. 1899 Wycombe (H) 4-1
1000
Moore, Tranter, Dunn, Hird, McEwan, McEachrane, Reynolds, J Reid, Lloyd, Gresham, Leonard
Scorers:- McEwan, Lloyd 2, OG 1

21. 01. 1899 Wolverton (A) 4-3
200
Moore, Tranter, Dunn, Dove, Chisholm, McEachrane, Reynolds, Hird, Lloyd, Gresham, Leonard
Scorers:- Dove, Chisholm, Leonard 2

28. 01. 1899 Chesham (H) 8-1
2000
Moore, Dunn, Tranter, Dove, McEachrane, Hird, Leonard, Gresham, Lloyd, J Reid, Reynolds
Scorers:- Lloyd, Reid, Reynolds 2, Dove, McEachrane, Gresham 2

11. 02. 1899 Brentford (A) 2-0
2000
Moore, Tranter, Dunn, Dove, Chisholm, McEachrane, Reynolds, J Reid, Henderson, G. Reid, Leonard
Scorers:- Reynolds, Leonard

18. 02. 1899 Uxbridge (H) 4-0
1500
Moore, Tranter, Dunn, Hird, Dove, McEachrane, Reynolds, J Reid, G. Reid, Henderson, Leonard
Scorer:- Henderson 4

04. 03. 1899 Southall (A) 2-0
4000
Moore, Tranter, Dunn, Chisholm, Dove, McEachrane, Reynolds, J Reid, Henderson, G. Reid, Leonard
Scorer:- Henderson 2

11. 03. 1899 St. Albans   (H)   1-0
2000
Moore, Tranter, Dunn, Chisholm, McManus, McEachrane, Hird, J Reid, Henderson, G. Reid, Leonard
Scorer:- J Reid

18. 03. 1899 Wolverton   (H)   2-1
1000
Moore, Tranter, Dunn, Chisholm, McManus, McEachrane, Hird, J Reid, Henderson, G. Reid, Leonard
Scorer:- J Reid 2

25. 03. 1899 Southall   (H)   2-0
3000
Moore, Tranter, Dunn, Dove, McManus, McEachrane, Hird, Bird, Henderson, G. Reid, Gilmore
Scorers:- G. Reid, Gilmore

08. 04. 1899 Fulham   (A)   1-0
3000
Moore, Tranter, Dunn, Chisholm, McManus, McEachrane, Hird, Lloyd, Henderson, Gresham, Leonard
Scorer:- Lloyd

15. 04. 1899 Maidenhead   (A)   10-0
3000
Moore, Tranter, Dunn, Chisholm, McManus, McEachrane, Hird, Lloyd, Henderson, J,Reid, Leonard
Scorers:- Lloyd 3.   Leonard 4, J Reid 2, Henderson

Championship Decider 1898/99
(played at Millwall)

22. 04. 1899 Cowes   3-1
1000
Moore Tranter, Dunn, Chisholm, Dove, McEachrane, Reynolds, Lloyd, Henderson, J Reid, Leonard
Scorers:- Lloyd, Henderson, Leonard

Test Match (play off) 1898/99
(played at Chatham)

29. 04. 1899 Sheppey Utd   1-1
2000
Moore, Tranter, Dunn, Chisholm, McManus, McEachrane, Reynolds, Lloyd, Henderson, Gresham, Leonard
Scorer:- Lloyd

Southern League Division 2
Final Table 1898-99

	P	W	D	L	F	A	Pts
Thames Ironworks	22	19	1	2	64	16	39
Wolverton	22	13	4	5	88	43	30
Watford	22	14	2	6	62	35	30
Brentford	22	11	3	8	59	39	25
Wycombe Wan.	22	10	2	10	55	57	22
Southall	22	11	0	11	44	55	22
Chesham	22	9	2	11	45	62	20
St Albans	22	8	3	11	45	59	19
Shepherds Bush	22	7	3	12	37	53	17
Fulham	22	6	4	12	36	44	16
Uxbridge	22	7	2	13	29	48	16
Maidenhead	22	3	2	17	33	86	8

Players appearances:- (including Championship Decider & Test Match):
Roddy McEachrane 24, Tommy Moore 23, Walter Tranter 22, Henry Hird 19, Simon Chisholm 17, Charlie Dove 15, George Gresham 15, James Reid 14, J. Reynolds 14, Tommy Dunn 13, David Lloyd 13, Pat Leonard 12, R. Henderson 10, A. Margeram 8, L. McEwan 8, Sam Hay 6, Peter McManus 6, George Reid 6, Alf Hitch 3, F. Adams 2, W. Atkinson 2, R. Cobb 2, Robert Hounsell 2, George Neil 2, Dick Bird 1, Brett 1, Buller 1, L. Foss 1, Henry Gilmore 1, Wenham 1

Goal Scorers:- (incl Decider & Test Match) Lloyd 12, J. Reid 9, Henderson 7, Leonard 7, Reynolds 5, Gresham 4, Dove 3, Hird 3, Atkinson 2, Hay 2, McEwan 2, Adams 1, Chisholm 1, Gilmore 1, Hounsell 1, McEachrane 1, G. Reid 1, Wenham 1, OG 1.

F.A. Cup 1898/99

01. 10. 1898 R E T B   (H)   2-0
1000
Moore, Tranter, Lloyd, Chisholm, Neil, McEachrane, Hird, Hay, Gresham, Adams, Cobb
Scorers:- Gresham, McEachrane

15. 10. 1898 Brighton Utd   (A)   0-0
2000
Moore, Dove, Tranter, Chisholm, Hitch, McEachrane, Lloyd, Hird, Adams, Gresham, Cobb

19. 10. 1898 Brighton Utd   (H)   1-4
2000
Moore, Dove, Tranter, Chisholm, Hitch, McEachrane, Lloyd, Hird, Adams, Gresham, Cobb
Scorer:- Hird

Thames & Medway Combination 1898/99

01. 09. 1898 Sheppey Utd   (A)   0-1
Moore, Tranter, Margeram, Chisholm, McEwan, McEachrane, Foss, Adams, Atkinson, J Reid, Hird

03. 09. 1898 Spurs   (A)   0-3
Moore, Tranter, Margeram, Chisholm, McEwan, McEachrane, Foss, Hay, Atkinson, J. Reid, Hird

07. 09. 1898 New Brompton   (A)   1-4
Rafter, Tranter, Margeram, Dove, Lloyd, McEachrane, Hird, Brett, Hay, Gresham, Foss
Scorer:- Brett

13. 09. 1898 Gravesend   (A)   2-5
Moore, Lloyd, Margeram, McEachrane, Neil, Barker, Hird, Hay, Atkinson, Gresham, Cobb
Scorers:- Hird, Gresham

06. 10. 1898 Chatham   (H)   1-2
Att. 500
Rafter, Tranter, Lloyd, Dove, Hay, McEachrane, Foss, Davies, Adams, Gresham, Cobb
Scorer:- Adams

22. 10. 1898 Grays Utd   (H)   2-0
Rafter, Tranter, Dove, Chisholm, Hitch, McEachrane, Reynolds, Adams, J Reid, Gresham, Buller
Scorers:- Gresham, Buller

16. 11. 1898 Chatham   (A)   0-1
Att. 500
Moore, Tranter, Margeram, Dove, McEwan, Chisholm, Hird, J Reid, Lloyd, Gresham, McEachrane

19. 11. 1898 R E T B   (A)   1-0
Moore, Tranter, Margeram, Dove, McEwan, Chisholm, Hird, J Reid, Lloyd, Gresham, McEachrane
Scorer:- McEachrane

10. 12. 1898 Dartford   (H)   1-0
Moore, Tranter, Margeram, Dove, McEwan, Chisholm, Hird, J Reid, Reynolds, Hay, McEachrane
Scorer:-Reid

07. 01. 1899 Grays Utd   (A)   2-1
Moore, Marjeram, Neil, Hird, Chisholm, McEachrane, Reynolds, Hounsell, Lloyd, J Reid, Gresham
Scorer:- Lloyd 2

02. 02. 1899 Gravesend   (H)   2-1
Moore, Tranter, Dunn, Hird, Dove, McEachrane, Reynolds, Allan, Lloyd, J Reid, Leonard
Scorers:- Reynolds, Lloyd

16. 03. 1899 Spurs   (H)   2-1
Moore, Tranter, Dunn, Dove, McManus McEachrane,
Hird, J Reid, Henderson, G. Reid, Leonard
Scorers:- Hird, J Reid

01. 04. 1899 R E T B   (H)   2-1

Moore, Tranter, Margeram, Chisholm, McManus, McEachrane, Hird, Lloyd, Henderson, J Reid, Gilmore
Scorers:- Hird, Lloyd

03. 04. 189 Dartford   (A)   2-1
Moore, Tranter, Harper, Chisholm, McManus, McEachrane, Hird, Lloyd, Henderson, J Reid, Gilmore
Scorers:- Lloyd, Henderson

06. 04. 1899 New Brompton   (H)   1-2
Moore, Tranter, Dunn, Dove, McManus, McEachrane,
Reynolds, Gresham, Lloyd, Henderson, G. Reid
Scorer:- Lloyd

20. 04. 1899 Sheppey Utd   (H)   3-2
Moore, Tranter, Dunn, Chisholm, Dove, McEachrane,
Lloyd, Reynolds, Henderson, J Reid, Leonard
Scorers:- Henderson, J Reid 2

Thames & Medway Combination
Final Table 1898-99

	P	W	D	L	F	A	Pts
New Brompton	16	12	2	2	48	14	26
Chatham	16	12	1	3	39	11	25
Gravesend	16	11	0	5	48	21	22
Tottenham Hotspur	16	10	0	6	43	28	20
Thames Ironworks	16	9	0	7	22	25	18
Sheppey United	16	7	1	8	31	31	15
Royal Engineers	16	3	2	11	24	55	8
Grays United	16	2	2	12	11	34	6
Dartford	16	2	0	14	21	68	4

Player appearances:- Roddy McEachrane 16, Walter Tranter 14, Tommy Moore 13, Henry Hird 12, James Reid, 12, David Lloyd 11, Simon Chisholm 10, Charlie Dove 10, Arthur Margeram 9, George Gresham 8, J. Reynolds 6, Sam Hay 5, R. Henderson 5, L. McEwan 5, Tommy Dunn 4, L. Foss 4, Peter McManus 4, F. Adams 3, W. Atkinson 3, Patrick Leonard 3, H. Rafter 3, R. Cobb 2, Henry Gilmore 2, George Neil 2, George Reid 2, Robert Allan 1, C. Barker 1, Brett 1, Buller 1, C. Davies 1, Harper 1, Alf Hitch 1, Robert Hounsell 1

Goal Scorers:- Lloyd 6, J Reid 4, Hird 3, Gresham 2, Henderson 2, Adams 1, Brett 1, Buller 1, McEachrane 1, Reynolds 1

Friendly matches 1898/99

17/09/1898	1st Coldstream Guards	H	2-0
19/09/1898	Woolwich Arsenal	A	0-4
26/09/1898	Millwall	A	0-0
12/10/1898	London Caledonians	H	2-1
29/10/1898	BarkingWoodville	A	1-1
03/11/1898	Millwall	H	1-1
10/11/1898	QPR	A	6-0
12/11/1898	Leytonstone	H	3-2
08/12/1898	Woolwich Arsenal	H	1-2
27/12/1898	New Brompton	H	1-1
04/02/1899	Wellingborough	H	5-0
25/02/1899	Eastbourne	A	3-1
23/03/1899	South Essex League	H	1-0

Motorcyclists at the Memorial Grounds

The cycling track

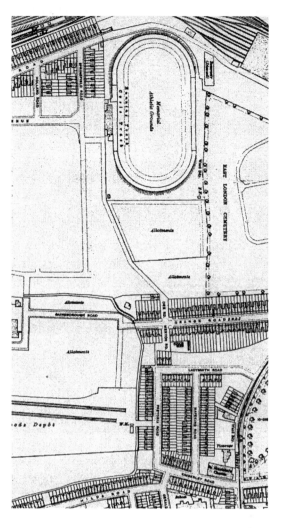

The site of the Memorial Grounds. The Hermit Road ground was situated at the bottom of the map, on the area later covered by Ladysmith Road and Kimberly Road.

CHAPTER SIX
THE FINAL WHISTLE
1899/1900

The close season of 1899 was to be a busy one for the club and nothing if not controversial. Now that the club were in a higher league the pool of players available needed to be improved with men of greater quality and experience. Francis Payne, the club's Secretary was given a large amount of money to procure the right players. Unfortunately he used the services of an agent (and professional footballer) by the name of Charlie Bunyan. Charlie had had something of a chequered playing career, for he was the Hyde United goalkeeper when they were defeated by a record 26-0 against Preston in the F.A. Cup back in 1887. He nevertheless survived to appear for several clubs, notably Derby County and Walsall, although at the latter club he once conceded twelve goals in a Second Division match on Boxing Day 1896, although to be fair Walsall played the whole match with just eight men! To allay any suspicions of his ability he conceded just 30 goals in 24 matches when he was an ever-present at New Brompton in 1898/99.

In his capacity as an agent he was requested to meet a particular player in Birmingham but he missed the appointment. Charlie tried to make amends by attempting to lure another player to the club with an underhand payment. The Birmingham association discovered the illegal approach and Charlie was summoned to appear before the F.A. It came to light that the money that was given by Arnold Hills to Francis Payne was being misused to persuade players to come to play for the Ironworks without the use of the authorised channels. Bunyan was suspended by the F.A. for two years and with that ban, his career, both as a player and an agent, was over.

As for Francis Payne, he failed to attend the F.A. hearing and was suspended until he did. A suspension was also handed out to Thames Ironworks FC for two weeks beginning on September 1st and the club was fined £25. Payne resigned as Secretary and was eventually banned by the F.A. for 'involvement in the poaching of players and financial irregularities' for twelve months from January to December 31st 1900. A quote from a local newspaper at the time stated, correctly, if a little dramatically, that 'Francis Payne is banned until the next century.'

It was a hefty disappointment and a total embarrassment to Arnold Hills. He must have rued the day that he agreed to accept the idea of the club turning professional and in addition he would have felt let down by his trusty lieutenant, Francis Payne. The fiasco would confirm any previous misgivings he had regarding the increasing financial responsibilities of the club as a professional outfit. After all, what had begun as just another sporting section of the Social and Athletic club, was now taking up the funds of the whole of that organisation.

With the resignation of Francis Payne, George Neil, the club's much respected full-back took over the reins as Club Secretary. He got down to the business of signing players as a matter of urgency and Albert Carnelly, a big strong forward, who had had Football League experience with Nottingham Forest and Leicester Fosse was signed from Bristol City. Neil's biggest coup however, came with the signing of three very experienced and proven goalscorers from 'Spurs, in Billy Joyce, Kenny McKay and Harry Bradshaw. With the shame of the F.A. hearing and a £25 fine on Hills' mind, Neil's first attempt to obtain approval from him to sign these players was rejected, but Neil eventually convinced Hills of the benefits of the quality of the additions to the club.

Two more players were brought to the club by George Neil. From New Brompton came Syd King, a full-back with a good pedigree, who was later to become Secretary and Manager of West Ham United, and Charlie Craig, who began his career in his native Scotland with Dundee. He came to London and was originally working at the Tates Sugar Refinery in Silvertown when Neil signed him. He worked as a marine boilermaker in his occupation at the yard and did not become a full-time professional until the 1901/02 season. Charlie Craig and Syd King formed a formidable full-back partnership with West Ham United for two seasons, and strangely enough both died on the same day in 1933.

There was concern and much disappointment that the proposed railway station at Manor Road, West Ham, which was to be situated right on the doorstep of the Memorial Grounds, would not be completed for the new campaign, and indeed it did not open until almost eighteen months later in January 1901. In view of this, and with the prospects of larger attendances due to the club's promotion to the Southern League Division One, arrangements were made by the committee with local bus and brake proprietors to run transport to and from the ground from Canning Town and Stratford Market stations.

At the club there were changes to the training staff where Sam Wright, who arrived from New Brompton, became head trainer, possibly on the recommendation

of Syd King, with Jack Ratcliffe dropping down to his assistant. Jack had previously replaced Tom Robinson for the 1898/99 campaign, after Tom had been the Ironworks trainer from the start and had originally been involved with the Old St Luke's, and later Castle Swifts clubs.

Tom however, despite his lack of direct involvement as trainer for a period of time, often invited a number of players from both the Ironworks and then West Ham United for breakfast at his home in Benledi Street, Poplar. Whether the fare provided was of any benefit when they took the field is not known, but Tom must have been a popular man at the time. He was of course, there or thereabouts at the Ironworks being involved with the training of cyclists at the Memorial Grounds and with local boxers. After his 'break' away

Tom Robinson

from football duties he returned as West Ham United's trainer at the age of 55, in 1904/05, the club's first season at their new Boleyn Ground, Upton Park. He remained with the club until 1912 when in gratitude for his services he was granted a testimonial match against QPR.

Training at the time was not quite what it is today. On the Monday following a match, a good brisk walk would be arranged to tone up the muscles and free up stiff joints. A period would be set aside for running, and sprinting for those who needed to improve their speed over short distances. With their facilities at the new ground the Irons had an indoor centre where skipping and the use of a punchball was considered good exercise and the use of Indian clubs (weights) was essential for strengthening the upper body. Actual training with the ball was not given great priority. It tended to be along the lines of the school playground game of '3 goals and in' with a goalkeeper and three defenders attempting to keep seven attackers at bay! When these activities were over the Irons' players were fortunate that the club had modern plunge baths and were able to receive a body massage to complete their training.

Whilst the club trainer was responsible for the physical fitness of the players, there was very little attention paid to the tactical side of the game. When players took the field for a match, they played in their allotted positions; if things went well and confidence grew teamwork usually fell into place. The responsibilities of the manager/secretary of the time chiefly concerned matters of an administrative nature and had little to do with team training. This is very different from the manager of today, who is a track-suited individual with a profile often as high as his top players and whose duties cover a whole range of functions including coaching, training, team tactics, administration, transfers and liaison with the Board, all conducted under the constant eye of the media. The modern manager is ultimately deemed responsible for his club's results, whether his players perform or not. He cannot be compared to his counterpart of 100 years ago.

Thames began their Southern League First Division campaign with an away match at Reading, a club that had been members of the league since its inception in 1894/95. With the new players in the team the Ironworks were expected to do well, so much so that the local Reading press indicated that any club could raise a decent team with the necessary finance behind them. However, despite some good performances from Carnelly and Bradshaw up front, Dove at half back, and Dunn in defence, it was the home side that won the day by a solitary goal, although the Irons more than held their own.

The club's first home fixture came on the following Monday evening with Chatham being the visitors. Season ticket prices were now 10/6d for the grandstand and enclosure, and 7/6d for rest of the ground. There was certainly no great rush to see the match as the attendance was just 1,000, which was a pity because Thames, after a battling and very even first half, ran out easy winners by four clear goals with McKay and Carnelly both grabbing two apiece.

The Ironworks next two Saturdays were taken up with the F.A. Cup. In the preliminary round the club had been drawn away to the Army side, Royal Engineers, who in the early years of the competition had been one of the leading clubs. They requested a change of venue for the match by foregoing ground advantage and it was switched to the Memorial Grounds where the Irons destroyed the opposition to the tune of 6-0, with Billy Joyce netting a hat-trick. A visit to Grays United in the next round saw the home side make a game of it in the first half, but although McManus missed a penalty, Thames then rattled in four goals to win the tie.

A rearranged Southern League away fixture against Brighton United was played during the following week, with Thames victorious by the slender margin of 1-0, although this result would be expunged before the end of the season due to Brighton's later demise. Four impressive victories brought an attendance of 3,000 to Canning Town for the visit of Bedminster who were unbeaten in the league and appeared a strong, burly outfit. The Irons, much to everyone's surprise, were all over their opponents right from the start and had their shooting been as good as their approach work, would have won by more than a solitary goal scored from a penalty by Joyce.

'Old Stager', the local correspondent, did have one gripe, however, stating (rather amusingly) that *Really, it is time that Association players dropped the habit of shouting out directions which is meant for advice, but can hardly be called such. Often a player is bewildered by cries of 'shoot', 'to the right', 'to the left', when had he been allowed to play his own game something tangible might have resulted; but instead, he generally makes a hopeless muddle in attempting to follow the advice from all parts of the field.'

Sheppey United provided the opposition in the F.A. Cup Second Qualifying Round, with Carnelly and Joyce grabbing two goals each in a 4-2 victory, and ten days later Sheppey were again the opposition when the Ironworks opened their

Thames & Medway Combination programme with a 3-3 draw on the Kent club's ground.

Thames were drawn away to Dartford in the next round of the F.A. Cup and overwhelmed the home side with a seven-nil victory. The local reporter of a Dartford paper, was almost certainly the same correspondent who wrote so critically of Thames Ironworks when the club visited Dartford almost four years to the day in 1895 with his remarks that meeting the club was '*lowering to the dignity of Dartford*'.

Now having to more or less 'eat his words', he could still not resist a number of derogatory remarks about Thames (and the club's supposed wealth) in his report of the match as follows: '*... no-one was greatly surprised at the 7-0 result. In these days the banking account has to be considered and the luxury of passing into the next round with little effort has proved an expensive one to the Ironworks. No more than 1400 were present and roughly speaking £30 was taken at the gate. Consequently the Thames share does not reach the wages bill, quite apart from the other expenses. Beaten though they were, it was obvious to everybody that Dartford elected to be defeated by fate, not by choice. Big names did not frighten them and although everybody napped the Works, Dartford made to make them go. The great margin is apt to convey the impression of a tame, not to say, one-sided game. But this was not so, and although there was skill and science on the one side, dash and grit were the marked features on the other.*

The Irons played the passing game with quick and accurate exchanges and there was no time to stop their defence which was on the Dartford men in a second. The home side committed a big mistake at the start. They made the pace too hot and for fully fifteen minutes the Ironworks faced the music. But by degrees Thames who had played a calm and steady game from the start, began to close in and goals began to come, and at half-time the score was 4-0 in their favour. Scorers were McKay, Carnelly (2) and McEachrane.

It was during the second half that pace began to take its toll. The Irons continued to play their game and three more goals were scored before the finish, from McKay, Bradshaw and Joyce. That the Works were far more superior is beyond all doubt. But the defeated are to be congratulated for making such a plucky show. The defence deserves special commendation for hard work.' (!!)

At the end of October Thames played Chatham in a Thames & Medway Combination match that ended in a 1-1 draw, which meant that the club were unbeaten in October and since the beginning of the season, in all competitions, had won seven matches, drawn two and lost just one, with 31 goals for and 7 against. Kenny McKay, Albert Carnelly and Billy Joyce had each scored eight goals apiece, proving what excellent acquisitions they had been. Everything was fine and the future looked promising, but within a few days the situation would not look so rosy.

Despite being little more than a stone's throw away from Thames old ground at Hermit Road, the actual location of the Memorial Grounds made it very difficult to access from a transport point of view and this would not improve until the proposed West Ham Station on the London to Tilbury line was built. The club committee did at least attempt to assist where they were able. For the Southern League fixture with 'Spurs, albeit an away match at White Hart Lane, arrangements were made to run horse brakes and buses to and from Canning Town as a large crowd of supporters were to travel with the team. The club may not have had tremendous crowds in those early days, but they did have a hard core of enthusiastic supporters.

The game with 'Spurs had been eagerly awaited, especially with the three former 'Spurs players being in the Thames team. There was a large contingent of Irons fans present, despite the heavy and persistent rain that turned the pitch into a quagmire. The local Ironworks correspondent jokingly stated *'it's a good job some of our men can swim, for the water and mud was pretty thick.'* He continued *'By the time the game had been in progress for half an hour the combined state of mud and water had transformed the players into dirt-bespattered figures, hardly distinguishable but for the once bright colours of the jerseys.'*

The game was fairly even to begin with, but it was noticeable that the Irons' forwards were not playing with the usual flow of recent matches and 'Spurs got on top, with Moore having to be at his very best to stem the tide. Joyce and Bradshaw combined well on one occasion and the home keeper had to make a save, but this was about the only time that the Irons looked dangerous in the first half during which 'Spurs scored twice.

The awful conditions affected the visitors more than 'Spurs but Carnelly had a much better half being denied by Waller in the home goal after two brilliant runs, but it was Thames defence that were having to hold out which they did until twenty minutes from the end when the third goal went in. The turning point between an ordinary defeat and a downright thrashing came straight afterwards when Dunn, who had played well in defence received an injury and had to retire. With both Joyce and McManus limping with knee injuries the Ironworks side collapsed and a further four goals were conceded.

The Thames committee and the supporters could not believe such a defeat, which caused quite some controversy and not a little bad feeling. On the Monday following the match the correspondent of the 'Morning Leader' stated *'In conversation with Mr Hills, Chairman of the Ironworks, I understand that the disaster to the team at Tottenham needs explanation. In the first place the pitch was unplayable. Several of the Committee men are of the opinion that the game should never have been started, and a protest is spoken of. At the conclusion, the Works supporters were amazed to learn that a league match had been played and not a friendly. It was thought that the referee ought to have examined the studs on the 'Spurs boots, and judging by the number of cuts and bruises there must have been something wrong. The following is a list of the injured:- Dunn, ricked hip, cuts and bruises; Joyce, three deep wounds on the right knee; McManus, knees badly cut; Moore, serious injury to thumb; King, badly bruised. In fact there is hardly a man in the team who does not bear injuries.'* The newspaper's correspondent continued *'This is serious and demands explanation. For looking at the result—7-0—it is very evident that peculiar circumstances must have entered into the affray to have produced such a 'licking' as that which the Irons received.'*

In the event there was no protest and the result stood, which is hardly surprising, but it is worth mentioning that Dunn, McManus and Joyce all missed the following two fixtures, one in the Thames & Medway Combination and one in the Southern League, but it was in the former match just two days later that the Irons, with five reserves in the team, and quickly wanting to make amends took it out on Grays United at the Memorial Grounds demolishing the Essex side and cruising to their biggest ever score in a victory by 11-1, with Carnelly scoring four and Bradshaw five goals.

There then followed three matches with New Brompton, one in the Southern League which, after all the recent goals, finished 0-0, with Moore saving a penalty. That score was repeated in the next round of the F.A. Cup, but in the replay Thames ran out winners by 2-0 with Tommy Moore again saving a penalty at a crucial moment in the game. The final game in November saw the Irons gaining a slender 1-0 home victory over Swindon Town. After the game the band played 'See the conquering heroes' and 'Let 'em all come', meaning Millwall, who were the next opponents in the F.A. Cup. So, despite the fiasco at White Hart Lane, Thames were still on course for a good season, but as is well known things can quickly change in football.

In an away encounter with Bristol City the Irons were forced to field several reserves, and with Carnelly, back on familiar territory, the only player playing up to form, the home side had a relatively easy 2-0 victory. Next up was the eagerly awaited F.A. Cup tie with near neighbours Millwall, and an enthusiastic crowd of 13,000, which would eventually be the best of the season, assembled at the Memorial Grounds. It was a very tight affair with the Ironworks forwards playing some first rate football along the ground, but the Millwall halves were equal to it, and the 'Lions' ran out winners 2-1, putting them into the First Round Proper of the competition. Carnelly and McEachrane were the pick of the Thames side, but the home crowd were criticized for lack of encouragement, when the Millwall supporters 'must have had cast iron lungs as they were shouting all afternoon.' This was unusual for the Ironworks crowd, because numbers may have not have been great but they were usually very vocal. Perhaps it was the visitor's early goal that disappointed, which gave Thames an uphill task from the start, but the chance of revenge against Millwall would come in a league match two weeks later.

Unfortunately, the team appeared to be suffering from a number of enforced changes that resulted in eighteen players being called upon during the month of December. Robert Allan, yet another Scot came down from Dundee and he became the regular outside right, but the club tried Adams, from Barking Woodville in defence and Walker from the local junior club Old St Luke's at outside left for a few games, and also gave a blooding to James Bigden also from Old St Luke's. However, these changes did nothing to improve the team's performance as a whole, and another blow came when the club visited Southampton and were beaten 3-1.

There was another large attendance, on this occasion 12,000, when Millwall made their league visit, but any thought of revenge quickly disappeared, when on a slippery pitch the visitors took a two goal lead by half-time. The Ironworks had managed to put the same players out for two consecutive games, but received two consecutive defeats after they were unable to pull the game round after the interval. However, during the second half the whole ground became enveloped in fog, and the game was abandoned 19 minutes from the end. What the Thames committee expected was that the match would have to be replayed but failed to confirm that this was the case. This error would rebound on them later in the season.

The holiday period was hardly one of celebration as not only did the Ironworks suffer another defeat, this time at the hands of Queen's Park Rangers on Christmas Day, but the club received the shocking news of the death of the team captain, Harry Bradshaw, on Boxing Day. This was completely unexpected, as he had not been seriously ill and had actually played in the cup-tie against Millwall, just over two weeks previously. What's more he had been a spectator at the 'Spurs versus Portsmouth match just twenty-four hours earlier. A close friend of Bradshaw was convinced that Harry died as a result of a succession of kicks received to the head whilst playing for Liverpool four years previously. As a consequence of this treatment the drum of his ear was severely damaged; the cause of his death was the rupture of a blood vessel in the brain. Those that knew Harry personally knew that he suffered at times particularly after heading a ball during a match and his only relief from pain was to press his hands to his ears. Despite this acute discomfort it came as a great shock to everybody that he had passed away. In fact the same friend had spoken to him only a couple of hours before he died and Harry had said that 'he was about all right again' and he hoped to play in the Irons next match. Bradshaw was just twenty-six years old and left a widow and two young children.

It must be remembered that the game in the 19th Century was far more physical, not to say violent at times, and remembering the phrase 'manly and robust' used by the F.A. no less, players were not protected by the stringent rules that exist today, whilst the treatment of injuries and aftercare were not of the same standard by any means.

From the purely cold and objective point of view of the club, Bradshaw was a valuable player to lose whatever the circumstances, particularly as the team were now dropping consistently down the league.

The return game with QPR was played at the Memorial Grounds four days after Bradshaw's death with the players all wearing black armlets. Maybe the team were affected by their colleague's demise as they under-performed again, losing by the odd goal in three, but there was growing criticism of the forwards inability to work as a unit and penetrate opposing defences. After all, despite recent defeats the defence had not been overwhelmed, but in the last eight league matches the forwards had scored just three goals.

There was also criticism once again in the local press about the general lack of vocal encouragement, with just the usual contingent being excepted. It is amusing to record the local correspondent's views during the above game: '...in advocating a little more cheering I did not expect what happened......At intervals during the game a chorus of about twenty voices felt it a duty to jerk—I say 'jerk' advisedly—out some encouragement to this effect: 'Pl-a-a-y up I-I-ron-wor-ks'. The voices were the nearest approach to that of a foghorn I have ever heard on the mainland. Such a distracting row, surely, was never intended to help our fellows on.' An early example of organised chanting and surely a forerunner of 'Come on you Irons'!

Thames had brought in two new players in December, Gilmore from Woolwich Arsenal and Turner from Brighton, but by the end of the season both players had appeared in only four games each. More productively, the following month saw the arrival of Frank Taylor from Harwich, a youngster with a great turn of speed, who was bought as a direct replacement for Harry Bradshaw. Much was expected of him and he missed only two Southern League matches until the end of the season, also playing in the remaining Thames & Medway Combination fixtures, but his early promise of becoming 'one of the greats' never materialised. In addition to Taylor, the Ironworks acquired the services of a very experienced half-back in William Stewart, yet another Scottish player, who had played for Dundee, Newton Heath (later re-formed as Manchester United), Luton Town and Millwall and he was to fill the centre of the half-back line spot, a problem position that had already been filled by four different players from the start of the season.

Both the above players made their debuts in the home match against Reading and although another defeat was registered (0-1), the Irons were very much on top and created several chances that should have been converted.

Three away fixtures followed, a 1-1 draw at Bristol Rovers was followed by a victory at last at Sheppey United by 3-0. This was nothing to be too euphoric about as the Kent club were bottom of the table, but a win is a win nevertheless. The third consecutive away game did not yield any further points however, when the Irons were defeated by Gravesend United 2-1.

It is perhaps appropriate that at this time the 'Athletic News' had a series of mottoes applied to various clubs with extracts from literary works. For Thames Ironworks FC they suggested lines from Shakespeare's 'King John':-

'When fortune means to men most good.
She looks upon them with a threatening eye'

Certainly an early rendering of 'Fortunes always hiding'!

Next up were Brighton United for the first match in February at the Memorial Grounds. After a heavy fall of snow that eventually turned the pitch into a quagmire, Thames ran out winners by 2-1, but this was against another very poor side. Brighton's financial situation was equally as poor because before the end of the season the Sussex club were forced to withdraw from the league. Despite being members of the Southern League, which was considered the most prestigious competition after the Football League, Brighton United's ground did not possess a main stand or any covered accommodation, and this contributed to their financial downfall. The winter of 1899/1900 was a particularly wet one and all Brighton's home games took place in rainy conditions which badly affected their attendances. Their eventual withdrawal had a double 'whammy' effect on the Ironworks because not only did it mean that all Brighton's results were expunged from the records, but having beaten Brighton both at home and away the Irons would have four points deducted from their total.

At this point it is significant to go back over six months to June 1899 when Arnold Hills wrote in the Thames Ironworks Gazette that: *'...in the development of our clubs, I find another tendency at work which seems to be exceedingly dangerous. The committees of several of our clubs, eager for immediate success, are inclined to reinforce their ranks with mercenaries. In our bands and in our football clubs, I find an increasing number of professionals who do not belong to our community but are paid to represent us in their several capacities...Now this is a very simple and effective method of producing popular triumphs. It is only a matter of how much we are willing to pay and the weight of our purses can be made the measure of our glory. I have however, not the smallest intention of entering upon a competition of this kind: I desire that our clubs should be spontaneous and cultivated expressions of our own internal activity...'*

This was an extraordinary statement to make bearing in mind Arnold Hills' agreement, just two months later, to the signing of professional players such as Carnelly, Joyce, McKay and Bradshaw. It is even more puzzling as Hills, at this time, was also negotiating to buy out the engineering company of John Penn, and it makes it more difficult to understand why, after making such a firm stand against an influx of football 'mercenaries' he agreed to take on the extra financial outlay for the football club, when he had to find money to fund a takeover. Perhaps, after having been convinced by others and despite his moral stance, he considered that if the wherewithal was provided and a successful team was the outcome, it would prove to be a profitable option.

Whatever his reasons Hills took up the same theme at the annual dinner of the Ironworks Federated Clubs six months later in February 1900, and the message was: *'It is necessary in some branches of sport to have professional representatives, because in no other way could the needs of the present time be met, but I do not attach great value to the professional aspect of sport — I rather desire to see amateur spirit associated with the clubs, inasmuch as I regard the clubs as opportunities for one and all of the young men associated with the works to obtain a good deal of muscular development, and a good deal of healthy recreation, and not to put it as a principle of gain.'*

Hills had begun by appearing to excuse himself for accepting the principle of professional players, but it was becoming increasingly obvious that he was gearing up to draw away from the financial responsibility of keeping the club afloat. Indeed by the end of February with the team gaining just one point from three matches, meetings had taken place and proposals made between Arnold Hills and the committee over the club's future.

In the 'West Ham Guardian' of 7th March 1900 it was reported that *'...it is announced that the committee of Thames Ironworks FC are to consider some sort of reorganisation. A proposal is evidently on the table. For one who has it on authority says it will 'if adopted, undoubtedly be to the club's advantage.' This is good news. Supporters are tired of seeing the club so low down as fourth from the bottom.'*

The real deciding factor of course was the Company's decision to buy out the engineering company of John Penn & Sons during the late summer of the previous year. In so doing, with the firm becoming a public company, Hills was obliged to raise capital making him responsible to shareholders of the new company with its full name of Thames Ironworks, Shipbuilding & Engineering Company Limited. He must have regretted his eventual agreement with football secretary George Neil, prior to the 1899/1900 season, regarding the addition of extra professional players to the club.

What might have, at that time, appeared a reasonable gamble on success was proving a failure. As the campaign had progressed, and other professionals had joined the club, it was obvious that with results so poor and attendances at the Memorial Grounds so low, it would be time to pull away from such a loss making exercise, with its drain on finances. With Hills now being accountable to shareholders, pumping more money into a club without any prospect of profit would be financial madness with the football club taking more money to run than all the other social organisations within the company put together.

After the victory over Brighton, which was to be of no use to Thames' league position whatsoever, due to the Sussex clubs eventual withdrawal from the league, the Irons gained just one point from the three remaining games in February, with Syd King receiving a booking for 'misconduct' in the 0-2 defeat against Portsmouth at Fratton Park. This was the Hampshire club's first season in any league, where they finished as runners-up, winning all their fourteen home matches in the process.

On 1st March Sheppey United visited Canning Town in the Thames & Medway Combination. Before the match, because the country was now involved in the Boer War in South Africa, the spectators, the referee and players sang the National Anthem. The visitors were thrashed 5-1 with young Taylor grabbing a brace, and by the end of the season Thames finished up in a respectable halfway position in that competition. The Southern League First Division however, was still proving to be hard going. The return match with 'Spurs took place with the Irons hoping for revenge for the debacle at White Hart Lane, but in a feeble encounter, which disappointed the crowd of 9,000, a 0-0 draw was the final score. The worst aspect of the match was that Syd King was taken to hospital after suffering a broken ankle and did not play again until the club became West Ham United the following season.

During March there was a court action brought against Thames Ironworks by the wife of Frank McCulloch, an employee, who had died at the Works. McCulloch was also an amateur footballer who had appeared for the Ironworks reserves and several other clubs in the area. (A pen picture is included at the end of the chapter). It was reported that Mrs McCulloch, of 25 Clifford Road, Canning Town, on behalf of herself and her four children, sued Thames Ironworks for £257 damages for the loss of her husband. The action was brought under 'The Workers Compensation Act'. Mr Goat, for the applicant, said that on the 29th November 1899 the deceased was at work in the Ironworks factory operating an iron-planing machine. While working, by some means, he got caught between the moving plane and the upright of another moving machine with the result that he received such injury that he died shortly after.

Mr Willis for the defence, submitted that respondents were not liable inasmuch as deceased had been guilty of serious and wilful misconduct. He had no business to be oiling the machine whilst it was in motion. His Honour, however, held that there was no evidence of wilful misconduct and awarded £257 to Mrs McCulloch, around £16,000 at today's values. It seems more than a little surprising that Thames Ironworks contested this action considering Arnold Hills' reputation for the welfare of his employees and their families.

On the field of play the Ironworks were still struggling. A rare home victory was recorded when Gravesend were beaten by 2-1 on a very windy day, with Carnelly scoring twice, but this was sandwiched between two defeats, both by the same score of 1-3. In both games Thames players could not even get on the scoresheet as the goals were 'own goals'. In fact in the months of February and March 1900 with just five goals netted in a total of seven Southern League matches, Carnelly, with three, was the only player to score, the others being those two own goals.

Joyce's lack of goals was redeemed in the first match in April when he scored twice against Portsmouth at Canning Town. Sad to say, the visitors popped in four in reply. On Easter Saturday Bristol City were the opposition in a scoreless draw on turf that was reported to be in good order 'despite the lateness of the season'. The quality of the pitch could not therefore be blamed for several mediocre home performances, but the Irons did themselves proud on Easter Monday when F.A. Cup Finalists Southampton visited the Memorial Grounds and were soundly beaten 4-1 with Bill Joyce grabbing a hat-trick and being carried shoulder high at the end of the game. The visitors may have been holding something back in view of the impending final, but it was a solid victory with Thames even having the luxury of missing a penalty. There were scenes of jubilation at the end of the match, but with just two games left to play the Ironworks were still in the relegation area, needing to win them both and also hoping that the teams just above, who were Chatham and Gravesend, would drop points.

Before those final two matches an announcement was made in the 'West Ham Guardian' as follows: *'The Ironworks supporters, says the 'Football Sun,' have for some weeks past been in low spirits. Ill-luck and bad gates account for the depression and there is a big balance on the wrong side of the treasurer's account to be faced at the end of the present season. This, however, will in all probability be wiped off by their generous president, Mr A. F. Hills. With regard to next season however, a meeting will be called, and the Mayor of West Ham will be asked to preside, at which gathering the locals will be asked to take up 500 £1 shares. If this amount be raised Mr A. F. Hills will add to it another £500, and, in addition, grant the use of the Memorial grounds. Another condition is that all the members of the team must be teetotallers. It is probable too, that the name of the club will be changed to Canning Town.'*

Would Arnold Hills' generous offer be forestalled not only by a lack of financial interest from members of the local business fraternity, but by several of a team of players succumbing to the odd alcoholic drink or two? Should the necessary finance be found, would the club reject a prospective team member, a forward with an exceptional scoring record, or a top-drawer defender because he had consumed a beer now and again? How could such a condition be monitored? Arnold Hills' obsession with the 'evils of drink' were admirable, but not necessarily practical.

From the financial viewpoint the local press were impressed by Arnold Hills' proposal. It was considered that if two thousand or more supporters each bought a share in the club it would be its salvation. The 'West Ham Guardian' stated, a little naively: *'There is little question that the present question of managing small teams is not the right one. For so many clubs get into debt and finally are snuffed out......A shareholder will have everything to gain, by attending the matches, and inducing others to come with him, therefore it seems to me that the nail has been hit right on the head, and the problem of the football world of management is about to be solved.'* It was not that simple. Many shares remained unsold for a considerable time. At first, however, it took the purchase of just ten shares to qualify as a member of the Board, but it was not easy going and for several seasons the finances of the new club were in a poor state. It was not until 1912 that a large loan and a considerable overdraft were settled, allowing the club to move forward. Any chorus from the terraces of 'sack the board' during that difficult period may well have been gratefully acted upon by the Chairman!

Meanwhile, in the relegation position along with Thames stood Sheppey United, who were defeated by four goals to two in the last home game of the season, the Irons' first and only double of the campaign.

Everything rested then on the final match of the Southern League season. It was against near-neighbours and rivals, Millwall, at East Ferry Road and the Thames had to win to stand any chance of First Division survival. Hundreds of Irons supporters made the short trip and despite the team bombarding the Millwall goal in the first half, the home side got on top in the second half and ex-Millwall keeper Tommy Moore had to be at his brilliant best to keep the opposition out. More importantly, however, Kenny McKay scored the winner for the Ironworks and should Chatham have lost their final match then the Irons would survive. If not, they would be involved in a Test Match with a team from the Second Division of the Southern League to decide who would be in the First Division the following season.

It will be remembered that when the home match in December was abandoned, Millwall were leading by 2-0, with the Southern League management deciding that the remaining 19 minutes would need to be played off. Had the Thames committee appealed in time the whole match would have had to be replayed, but this they failed to do until March and their late appeal was rejected. It is also possible that the Ironworks would have won, giving them an extra two points. As it was, a ridiculous situation arose when both teams were ordered to play off another 19 minutes of the December match after the 90 minutes of the current game was up. However, several of the Ironworks officials came on to the ground at the call of time and gave instructions to the team to refuse to play, and they left the field. Nevertheless the League mandate had to be obeyed and Mr Walker, the referee, visited the dressing room and after consultation with officials persuaded them to turn out again. The subsequent play was simply farcical, neither side caring to assert themselves. The Irons hadn't the slightest chance of pulling back two goals and Millwall were content as it was and both teams were glad at the finish. It meant, of course, that Thames had won and lost a game on the same afternoon.

In the event, Chatham did manage to win their final match, which meant that the Irons would have to take part in a Test Match (play-off). Their opponents were Fulham who had finished as runners-up in the Second Division, and the match was scheduled to be played just two days after the Millwall game, at neutral White Hart Lane.

The Irons had an unchanged team, and winning the toss they took advantage of the wind behind them. They were on the attack from the start and the Fulham defence were all over the place especially the left-back Howland who had a nightmare, mis-kicking on several important occasions and completely losing his head when scoring an own goal. He was at fault with at least two of Thames goals, but the defence as a whole were totally disorganised and hampered the rest of the team. This is not to take the credit away from the Irons forwards who were outstanding, especially Joyce who scored a hat-trick and Stewart who also scored. David Lloyd, the ex-Thames Ironworks player, was Fulham's best individual and scored their only reply, heading in a free-kick. Fulham were upset with the referee, who, they claimed made some dubious decisions including disallowing for offside what was considered to be a legitimate goal. However, there was no doubt whatsoever that Thames had won a convincing victory and that the best team won. It also meant that their Southern League First Division place was assured.

Nevertheless it is difficult to evaluate the reasons why Thames season overall proved to be nothing short of disastrous. Apart from the 0-7 reverse at Tottenham, which had a touch of controversy about it, the performances of the defence were more than adequate. Had that defeat not been so heavy the defence would have had a record that compared favourably with those near the top of the league. It was the lack of goals scored which was the main problem. The 30 scored was the second worst in the division, and although the three forwards signed during the close season scored 24 of them it was a poor return considering their undoubted ability. Criticism however, must be made of the half-backs, or what we would call today the 'midfield' players, for their contribution from a goalscoring point of view was non-existent, but on the other hand it is likely that the majority of their time was spent in defensive duties. Whatever the reason for the club's poor showing the whole side consisted of quality players, but they did not 'gel' to make a successful team.

In the Premier League of the 21st Century the majority of quality players are those from foreign shores, and they are paid accordingly. Some say, too much. There is not a great deal of loyalty and certain players are, without doubt, what can only be called mercenaries. In the last decade of the 19th Century the foreign players of the day were those of Scottish origin. They were usually quality players, they were well paid and a number of those were mercenaries.

In the season of 1895/96 First Division Sunderland used eighteen players overall. Seventeen of those were Scottish! Preston North End had nine Scots, Everton seven. Woolwich Arsenal had ten Scots and the remainder were not born in the south. As long ago as 1890 the magazine 'Pastime' wrote *The spectator does not care, whether his team or village team is composed of bona fide natives or Scotchmen hired from afar. Provided that they win their matches, he is well satisfied, and he never doubts that victory is creditable to the place with whose money it is won.'*

So it was generally understood that a team liberally sprinkled with players from North of the Border would usually be one of moderate success at least, providing they all bonded together. In 1898/99 Thames had Scotsmen Chisholm, McEachrane, McEwan, J. Reid, followed by Dunn, Leonard, G. Reid and McManus and those men all played their part in a successful season. However in the close season of 1899, Joyce, McKay and Craig and later in the campaign, Allan and Stewart, all Scots, were added to the squad. Together with Englishmen Carnelly and Bradshaw, who both had experience and were quality players, it would appear that skill in abundance had been brought to the club. Unfortunately, as very often happens, individual skill, although of importance, is not always the answer without the necessary teamwork to round it off – this certainly applied in recent times when West Ham United were relegated from the Premier League in 2002/03.

Of the nine Scottish players that the Ironworks fielded in the club's last season (seven of them on a regular basis), the two that disappointed most were Joyce and McKay. Together with Carnelly, who was an Englishman, they contributed a reasonable number of goals but there were many games when easy scoring opportunities were missed, and in others pretty footwork and concentration on combination play was overdone. When all is considered those three players took part in a considerable number of matches, since they were not only regulars in both the Southern League and the Thames & Medway Combination side, but were also chosen to play in the London League team at various times which was essentially a reserve competition. As an example, McKay played in the Southern League team against New Brompton on 17th March 1900, for the London League side against Monsteds Athletic on 19th March, in the T & M Combination against Grays United on 21st March and against Gravesend in the Southern League on 24th March. Four matches in eight days!

All three players moved on at the end of the season. Perhaps, due to their constant movement between clubs, they could be described as mercenaries, but it would be a little unfair as over many years of the history of football there is a constant traffic in players. Especially in today's world where loyalty is in short supply. After all, there are very few with the loyalty of the likes of Brooking, Devonshire and Martin around today!

Whatever the failings of the team during that final season, Thames Ironworks FC had gone out on a positive note by winning the very last match of their five-year existence and had laid the foundations for a new club to build upon should Arnold Hills' proposals come to fruition. It was most likely that should there be a positive outcome, the new club would take over where the Ironworks left off and be admitted into the First Division of the Southern League.

On the Saturday when the final game was due be played an article appeared in the 'Morning Leader': *The prospectus of the new limited liability company, to be known under the title of The West Ham Football Club Company Limited is at hand. The primary object will be to encourage and promote the game of football in West Ham and district, and powers have also been taken by the company authorising them at any time to acquire land and other property. The company has been constituted on the ordinary lines, except that by the rules of the English Football Association no dividend beyond 5 per cent per annum can be paid. The affairs will be managed by a board of directors.........The directors propose to make the following charges, to shareholders only, for season-tickets for the football season 1900/01: Admission to ground and open stand, 7s 6d, admission to ground, enclosure and grand stand 10s. The prices to non-shareholders for these season tickets will be 10s 6d and 12s 6d respectively. The Memorial Grounds at Canning Town will again be utilised, and we are glad to hear that the London, Tilbury and Southend railway station, West Ham, adjoining the grounds, is quite ready to be opened when required......The Great Eastern Railway also contemplate building a station facing the grounds, and the proposed municipal tramways will pass the entrance to the grounds. Mr A. F. Hills who will most likely take up £500 worth of shares, is very keen on playing a teetotal eleven next season, and the experiment is worth trying if only to vindicate the rights of football employers to call their own tune after paying the piper. There must be something remarkably timid, however, in the constitution of a football management that has to seek a remedy of this kind, and we shall watch the movements of the West Ham recruiting sergeant with great interest. One thing seems obvious — the anti-Bacchus side can scarcely get into a tighter place than that which brings its programme to a close this afternoon.'*

Arnold Hills could quite easily have broken all ties with the club and wound the whole thing up, and it says much for the character of the man that he did not. After all, he was not duty bound to give any further assistance, financial or otherwise. Of course, the Memorial Grounds were still there, standing as an example of a dream that would turn out to be a nightmare should the place become a 'white elephant'. The ground would still be used for cycling, cricket and athletic meetings of a more parochial nature but it would not retain its original impact as a sporting venue of some standing. He decided then, not to cut his losses and run, for he proposed a limited company, with himself as the major shareholder. The capital of West Ham United was £2,000, or 4,000 shares of 10s each, with Hills promising to buy one share for every one sold to the public, although some remained unsold two years later. As a consequence Thames Ironworks FC resigned from the Southern League and was wound up in late June 1900 and on July 5th West Ham United Football Club was registered as a company and was elected to take its place in the Southern League. An initial agreement was also made that the Memorial Grounds would be at the new club's disposal for a nominal rent for three years.

So ended the short but eventful existence of a Company football team that survived mainly because of the goodwill and generosity of one man, Arnold Hills, who would also be instrumental in the founding of its successor, West Ham United, a club that was to become well known, not to say famous, and one that for the most part played the game the way it should be played, even if the end result was not the one all Irons' fans would have liked.

Thames Ironworks 1899/1900. Back (players only); C Barker, A Woodcock, CT Craig, HS Sunderland, H Gilmore, FT Adams. Next to back; F Corbett, C Dove, T Dunn, S King, J Bigden, L Foss, M Higham, S Wright (trainer). Seated; WH James, K McKay, T Moore, A Carnelly, H Bradshaw. Front; J Walker, P McManus, W Joyce, R McEachrane, D Chisholm.

PEN PICTURES

Robert Allan *born Dundee Scotland, 1876*

Like Charlie Craig, Robert began his career at Dundee, once scoring a hat-trick from the wing in a Scottish F.A. Cup second round match against Kings Park in January 1897. Not always a regular in the Dundee side, he came to Thames Ironworks in 1899 and appeared in 22 consecutive matches in the Southern League including the Test Match and 7 consecutive in the Thames & Medway Combination in 1899/1900. He was one of the band of players who played for both Thames Ironworks and West Ham United making a further 52 appearances for the latter along with 5 F.A. Cup matches. Apart from his hat-trick in his early Scottish days Robert was not a goalscoring winger, managing only two goals during his stay. He was an unselfish player who was able to take hard knocks mainly due to his weight, which was well above average for a winger, although when he was converted into a half-back in 1900/01 this was a distinct advantage. Bob's weight was obviously down to his liking for doughnuts and toffee apples, and the breakfasts that he indulged in at ex-trainer Tom Robinson's house along with several other players of that period.

James Bigden *born Poplar, 1880*

James was a local lad who began playing in the junior side of the Old St Luke's club as a 13 year old where he continued until Thames Ironworks picked him up for the 1899/1900 season. A hard working and strong half-back at 5ft 8 in and 12 stone he appeared 11 times in the Southern League side, twice in the F.A. Cup, and on two occasions in the Thames & Medway Combination. At the end of the season however, when the club became West Ham United, he joined Gravesend United also of the Southern League, making 26 appearances for them and scoring once. West Ham then took him back for the following season of 1901/02 and he spent 3 seasons with them playing 91 times, scoring 3 goals in the Southern League and appearing on five occasions in the F.A. Cup before he took the eye of Woolwich Arsenal in the First Division of the Football League. During his time there he was a member of the team that knocked West Ham out of the F.A. Cup in 1905/06. Four seasons with the Plumstead club saw him make 75 appearances (one goal) before he took the long trip North in 1908/09 to play for Bury, also a First Division club at that time, but he was on the first eleven team sheet on only three occasions. He returned South the following season where he finished his career at Southern League side Southend United making just 4 appearances.

Thomas H. Bradshaw *born Liverpool August 24th 1873 Died December 25th 1899*

Born Thomas, but always known as Harry, he began his career at Northwich Victoria in 1892/93. A strong, direct winger with an eye for goal, he made an immediate impact scoring 8 goals from 18 appearances. The following campaign, after just 4 matches, he joined his home-town club, Liverpool, remaining with the club until the end of the 1897/98 season. During that time the team won the Second Division Championship twice, in 1894 and 1896. In all he made 118 league appearances for them, scoring 46 goals, a phenomenal average for a player who was essentially a winger. Harry represented the Football League on two occasions, and gained an England cap against Ireland in 1897. He then came south to join 'Spurs in 1898/99. In addition to 22 Southern League appearances (3 goals) he represented the United Counties League against the Thames & Medway Combination, The South v The North and played in the Players Union international when an English XI met a Scottish XI at Crystal Palace. The following season Harry arrived at Thames Ironworks along with two other 'Spurs players, McKay and Joyce. Set up by George Neil, the new club secretary, this was transfer coup if ever there was one, agreed after much original objection, due to cost, from Company Chairman Arnold Hills. In three competitions overall Bradshaw scored eight goals in 15 outings with recent research revealing that he scored 5 goals against Grays United in a Thames & Medway Combination match. His captaincy and general play proved to be badly missed after he collapsed and died on Christmas Day 1899. Harry had also been a useful cricketer, playing for a prominent club in Liverpool; he mentioned just a short time before his death that he was expecting to join the groundstaff at Lords for the 1900 season.

Albert Carnelly *born December 29th 1870 Died 1920*

Much-travelled Albert Carnelly, who was a big, strong, beefy forward, was not only a prolific goalscorer, but a first class dribbler. He was on Notts County's books and then Loughborough Town before making his debut at Nottingham Forest in 1894/95 where he scored 16 goals in 29 appearances and 8 goals from 23 matches the following season. In 1896/97 he joined Second Division Leicester Fosse for what was described as 'a big sum' and his goal tally there was 10 in 28 games. On to Southern League Bristol City for 1897/98 he found the net on no less than 27 occasions from 35 outings in two seasons, a phenomenal scoring rate. Perhaps now becoming known as a 'mercenary', he joined Thames Ironworks for the 1899/1900 season. The team struggled in the First Division of the Southern League and goals were hard to come by, but he performed creditably. In three competitions he scored an overall twenty goals in 44 matches. After just one season he was off to pastures new when he joined Millwall, also in the Southern League. In 13 appearances he scored twice, but the following season he finished his career at Midland League club Ilkeston Town. Albert was only 49 years old when he died in 1920.

Fred Corbett *born Stepney, August 1880*

A strong, hardworking inside forward, Freddy

joined Thames Ironworks from the junior side Old St Luke's at the same time as James Bigden in 1899/1900, playing just three times in the Southern League side, and once in the Thames & Medway Combination without scoring. He did however, play consistently for the reserves in the London League and was top scorer for them. When the club became West Ham United he blossomed and scored 13 goals in 33 appearances in the first team in two seasons before moving to Bristol

Rovers in 1902 scoring 6 goals in 26 appearances. The following season he moved to local rivals Bristol City who were in the Football League Division 2 at that time, where in two campaigns he made 49 appearances, scoring 16 goals. He was back in London with Southern League Brentford in 1905 scoring 39 goals in 81 matches over 3 seasons, but returned to Bristol Rovers in 1908 staying for 3 years and scoring 36 goals from 97 outings. One season with New Brompton in 1911 followed with 6 goals from 22 appearances. His final season of 1912/13 saw him in Wales with Merthyr Town where he played in just two first team matches in the Southern League without scoring.

Charlie Craig *born Dundee Scotland, July 11th 1874 Died 1933*

Charlie was a strong and reliable full back who began his career as a 19 year old at his local club Dundee in the first year of their formation in 1893/94, where he made 13 appearances. The following season saw him with Dundee Wanderers making eight appearances before returning to Dundee and a further 4 seasons service. His first team outings were limited, but he then came south to initially work for Tates Sugar Refinery at Silvertown and then to Thames Ironworks. He was employed there as a Marine Engine Fitter, but found himself in the Ironworks side immediately, although the majority of the team were professionals. He played 18 times in the Southern League, including a Test match, six times in the Thames & Medway Combination and on four occasions in the F.A. Cup. When Thames Ironworks became West Ham United he formed a formidable full-back partnership with Syd King and made 53 Southern League appearances and 7 in the F.A. Cup over two seasons. Turning full professional he joined First Division Nottingham Forest for 1902/03 and stayed at the club for five seasons making 137 appearances and scoring twice. He was not only described as a 'genial, good natured giant' but it was said that he was 'one of the most scrupulously fair players it would be possible to find.' Not only that, he was also an excellent athlete, winning medals for successes on the track.

He stepped down into the Southern League with Bradford Park Avenue in 1907/08 making 28 appearances but when the club were accepted into the Football League the following season he left after 6 matches and joined Norwich City, so it was back to the Southern League again. After 48 appearances there in two seasons, he made yet another move, this time to Southend United in 1910/11. Another 23 Southern League starts there, and yet another change of scenery the following season when Charlie was off to Wales where he joined Merthyr Town. They were in the Second Division of the Southern League at the time and he helped them to promotion. After two seasons in the top division with Charlie making 59 appearances it was April 1914, and time for him to call it a day. By now he was coming up for forty years of age and he had been 'kicking the leather' for 21 of them, with well over 400 appearances to his credit. This was a lengthy career by the standards of the day. He had begun his career in his native Scotland, continued to ply his trade in England, and finished up in Wales. A pity that he did not put pen to paper and describe his sporting experiences in the time of three monarchs; Victoria, Edward VII and George V. It is ironic that Charlie and Syd King, who formed a remarkable full-back partnership with West Ham United, should both die on the same day in 1933, albeit under vastly different circumstances.

In the period that Charlie Craig was at Thames Ironworks/ West Ham United he lived at 48 Tate Road, Silvertown, opposite the Sugar Refinery.

Henry Gilmore *born Berwick, circa 1877*

Was on Woolwich Arsenal's books until he joined Thames Ironworks in 1899. Always just on the fringe of the first team, he could play at either wing-half or left-wing. In 1898/99 he played just one game in the Southern League Division Two, scoring against Southall, and twice turned out for the Thames & Medway Combination. The following campaign he made 4 appearances in the Southern League Division One, and one in the T & M. He joined South West Ham and was still playing for them in 1903. Interestingly, he was employed at the yard as a shipbuilders timekeeper.

William Joyce *born Prestonpans Scotland, April 8th 1877*

Bill was a high scoring centre forward who began his career in Scotland with Morton in 1893/94. He joined First Division Bolton Wanderers for the following campaign where he went on to score 16 goals in 30 matches over three seasons. This average would have undoubtedly been higher as his games were limited due to a broken leg sustained in January 1895, which kept him out of action for just over twelve months. He moved on to the Southern

League with 'Spurs in 1897/98 where he scored an amazing 16 goals in 19 appearances followed by 10 from 19 in the next campaign. 1899/1900 saw him at Thames Ironworks where 21 goals in 44 matches in three competitions was a good return, almost the same as that of fellow team-mate Carnelly, but it was generally felt that his goal tally could have been even better as many chances went begging. Bill spent just the one campaign at Thames, leaving to join fellow Southern League side Portsmouth. Here, his scoring record, like that at 'Spurs, was outstanding as he found the net on 16 occasions from 21 matches. His last club was Football League Second Division side Burton United where, over two seasons from 1901/02 he scored 16 goals in 52 outings.

Syd King *born Chatham, 1873 Died 1933*

As much has already been written about the life and career of Syd King, mainly as Manager of West Ham United, a sketch of his playing days takes preference here with just a brief mention of his later life.

Syd began his career as a full-back with Northfleet in the Southern League in 1896/97, making 18 appearances. It was whilst he was playing for the 'Cementers' that he claimed to have scored a hat-trick of own goals in a match against Swindon. He may have emphasized this to conceal several incidents in the same match, for the truth is somewhat different. It is true that he scored one own goal, but not three. However, the game was very rough and rife with fouls. Apart from Syd's team-mate Pennington being sent off, King himself was said by the referee to have incited other players to misconduct and was also cautioned for using offensive language to an opponent. At the close of the game King also 'addressed an offensive remark' to the referee. In addition two spectators were ordered from the ground. At a subsequent F.A. disciplinary hearing both King and Pennington were suspended for a month. Syd joined New Brompton for the following campaign making 37 Southern League appearances for them in 2 seasons. He then came across the river to join up with Thames Ironworks in 1899 and formed a full-back partnership with Tommy Dunn, which went well until Syd broke his ankle against 'Spurs in early March 1900, and that put him out for the rest of the season. All in all he appeared in 29 first team matches in three competitions for the Ironworks. Playing for the new club of West Ham United Syd was part of a formidable full-back partnership, this time with the Scot Charlie Craig, which lasted for two full seasons and part of another, before King took on the full time responsibilities of Secretary and then Manager. For the record, between 1900/01 and 1902/03 he made 59 Southern League and seven F.A. Cup tie appearances. He did not score one league goal in his whole career, but he did score an own goal, but not three in one match!

He was instrumental in the club's move from the Memorial Grounds at Canning Town to the Boleyn Ground at Upton Park, and in 1906 wrote a very short history of the club. His management skills in guiding the club to promotion and the first ever F.A. Cup Final at Wembley is well documented. He remains the longest serving manager in the club's history (1902-1932), a record that is certain to stay. After such a long and successful association with the club, he was drunk and insubordinate at a club board meeting in November 1932 and he was suspended, a decision which was to ultimately lead to his suicide in January 1933.

On a lighter note, during the period of Syd's playing career at Thames there were several occasions when athletic challenges were arranged prior to matches of less importance. One such took place when West Ham United visited West Norwood for a friendly match in September 1901. A 75 yard handicap race had been set up by Baron von Reiffenstein, the home club's benefactor. Rainbird (West Norwood) and McEachrane (WHU) were to start at scratch, Syd was given two yards start and the Baron four yards. Apparently 'a good race followed'; Syd King came in first, McEachrane second, Rainbird third and the Baron last. It was said that 'for an old 'un' the Baron ran well!

Frank McCulloch *born 1868 Died November 1899*

One of a number of unsung players who played the game at local level on a strictly amateur basis and was employed at Thames Ironworks & Shipbuilding Company. Began his football career at Millwall in 1893/94 making several appearances in their first team. When Millwall became on of the founder members of the Southern League the following season Frank played in the reserve side only and then joined Old Castle Swifts playing regular first team football, appearing for them in their one and only venture into the F.A. Cup when they lost after a replay to Wolverton. He was not a tall player but one of stocky build, playing most of the time as a forward who was capable of scoring goals, as he proved by registering a hat-trick for Old Castle Swifts in February 1895 against King's College Hospital. After the collapse of Old Castle Swifts he appeared for Thames Ironworks but only in the reserve side, but he then joined St Luke's for the reminder of the 1895/96 season. In the latter part of that campaign Frank was involved in an incident in a South Essex League match against Leytonstone when he came into collision with Isern, the 'Stones goalkeeper, who received the full force of McCulloch's weight in the chest, but it was not until after the game was over that Isern was taken to hospital seriously ill, and he remained in that condition for some days until he eventually recovered. However, the Leytonstone executive reported McCulloch to the London Football Association and it was only after witness evidence that he was cleared.

Frank continued to play for St Luke's the following season and was in their team when they were defeated by Ilford in the F.A. Cup in November 1896. In the New Year the St Luke's club folded however, but he joined Manor Park in 1897/98 and played there for two seasons in the South Essex League. It was on to Commercial Athletic for the 1899/1900 season until he met his tragic death whilst using an iron-planing machine at Thames Ironworks in November 1899.

Frank McCulloch was residing at 25 Clifford Road, Canning Town with his wife and four children at the time of his accident.

Kenny McKay *born Wishaw Scotland, circa 1876*

Began his career at Hamilton Academicals before joining Sheffield United in 1896/97, appearing in just one game. The following season with them he gained a Football League First Division Championship medal making 25 appearances and scoring 5 goals. He joined Southern league outfit 'Spurs in 1898/99 contributing four goals in 17 matches. He was very much a foil for Billy Joyce, both at 'Spurs and Thames Ironworks, laying on many opportunities for his team-mate. Even so, he was capable of scoring on his own account notching up 16 goals in 46 matches in three competitions for Thames Ironworks in 1899/1900. Interestingly, in one match in the Thames & Medway Combination at Grays Utd, Kenny took up the goalkeeper's jersey, when Sunderland, the reserve keeper was unable to take Moore's place. After just one season at Thames he signed for Fulham, where he scored 22 goals in 50 competitive matches over two seasons and gained a Southern League Division Two Championship medal with them in 1902/03.

William S. Stewart *born Coupar Angus Scotland, February 11th 1872 Died June 1945*

His first club was Dundee Our Boys, but he came South and by the age of seventeen was playing for Newton Heath (later Man. Utd) in the newly formed Football Alliance in 1889 where he was an immediate success. Willie played in the centre of the half-back line, when the position was more mobile at that time, and not the defensive centre back that it is today. In the three seasons that Newton Heath were in the Alliance he missed just 4 matches from sixty-six. In 1892/93 the club were accepted into the Football League First Division, and a further three seasons saw him appearing 76 times and scoring 3 goals. When the club were relegated at the end of 1894/95 he moved on to Luton Town. He made 17 appearances and scored 4 goals in their Southern League side, but then the club moved to the United League where Willy helped them to runners-up spot. For the following season of 1897/98 the club were accepted into the Second Division of the Football League with Stewart making a strong contribution to the side, scoring 10 goals in 30 appearances. He returned to the Southern League the following season, on this occasion with Millwall, missing just one game in a 24-match programme and scoring one goal. Luton Town re-signed him for 1899/1900 and he made 15 appearances for them, but the club were struggling and eventually finished second from the bottom of the table and did not apply for re-election to the Football League. William however, had already left the club at the end of December and signed for Thames Ironworks playing in the final 17 matches of the Southern League season (including the Test match) and he also figured in the final five matches of the Thames & Medway Combination. He left before the club became West Ham United and returned to Dundee. Willie was also an excellent cricketer who played for Forfar and Perthshire.

Frank Taylor

Came from Harwich as a youngster in the final season of Thames Ironworks FC's existence. As a winger he was brought in to fill the left-wing position left vacant by the death of Harry Bradshaw. He was predicted to become 'one of the finest outside lefts in the kingdom' according to the club's handbook. Indeed, a local report of his first game when the Irons played Reading, stated *'Taylor is a surprising youth. He fairly delighted the spectators by his speed. There is promise in Taylor.'* One month later the local paper was at it again: *'Taylor was in good form and will supply an answer to the eager enquiries of his former friends as to how he is progressing. One can hardly change the constitution of a team, but Taylor has infused new life into the front rank...'*

Frank played 15 matches, scoring one goal in the Southern League and made 5 appearances in the Thames & Medway Combination, scoring twice in a 5-1 victory over Sheppey United. When the club became West Ham United he scored 4 goals in 12 outings in 1900/01, but during the following campaign he made just one appearance for the club scoring in an F.A. Cup tie against Leyton. Like a number of young players down the years at West Ham who have been heralded as 'wonder boys' with a star studded future he failed to live up to his early promise. In his case, he disappeared from the senior football scene altogether.

Southern League Div One 1899/1900

16. 09. 1899 Reading   (A)   0-1
3000
Moore, Dunn, King, Dove, McManus, McEachrane, Corbett, McKay, Joyce, Carnelly, Bradshaw

18. 09. 1899 Chatham   (H)   4-0
1000
Moore, Dunn, King, Dove, McManus, McEachrane, Corbett, McKay, Joyce, Carnelly Bradshaw
Scorers:- McKay 2, Carnelly 2

07. 10. 1899 Bedminster   (H)   1-0
3000
Moore, Dunn, King, Dove, McManus, McEachrane, Hird, McKay, Joyce, Carnelly, Bradshaw
Scorer:- Joyce

04. 11. 1899 Tottenham Hotspur   (A)   0-7
7000
Moore, Dunn, King, Dove, McManus, McEachrane, Craig, McKay, Joyce, Carnelly, Bradshaw

11. 11. 1899 New Brompton   (H)   0-0
2000
Moore, Craig, King, Gentle, Dove, McEachrane, Janes, McKay, Carnelly, J Reid, Bradshaw

25. 11. 1899 Swindon   (H)   1-0
2000
Moore, Dunn, King, Craig, Bigden, McEachrane, Adams, McKay, Joyce, Carnelly, Walker
Scorer:- Adams

02. 12. 1899 Bristol City   (A)   0-2
3000
Sunderland, Craig, King, Bigden, McManus, McEachrane, Corbett, McKay, Carnelly, Joyce, Walker

16. 12. 1899 Southampton (A) 1-3
4000
Moore, Craig, Adams, Dove, Bigden, McEachrane, Allan, McKay, Carnelly, Joyce, Walker
Scorer:- McKay

23. 12. 1899 Millwall (H) 0-2
12000
Moore, Craig, Adams, Dove, Bigden, McEachrane, Allan, McKay, Carnelly, Joyce, Walker

25. 12. 1899 Q P R (A) 0-2
4000
Moore, Craig, Adams, Gilmore, Bigden, McEachrane, Allan, McKay, Carnelly, Joyce, Walker

30. 12. 1899 Q P R (H) 1-2
4000
Moore, Craig, Adams, Gilmore, Turner, McEachrane, Allan, McKay, Carnelly, Joyce, Walker
Scorer:-McKay

06. 01. 1900 Chatham (A) 1-3
5000
Moore, King, Adams, Gilmore, Turner, McEachrane, Allan, McKay, Joyce, Carnelly, Walker
Scorer:- Carnelly

13. 01. 1900 Reading (H) 0-1
4000
Moore, Dunn, King, Bigden, Stewart, McEachrane, Allan, McKay, Joyce, Carnelly, Taylor

15. 01. 1900 Bristol Rovers (A) 1-1
6000
Moore, Dunn, King, Bigden, Stewart, McEachrane, Allan, McKay, Joyce, Turner, Taylor
Scorer:- McKay

20. 01. 1900 Sheppey Utd (A) 3-0
4000
Moore, Dunn, King, Bigden, Stewart, Craig, Carnelly, Joyce, McKay, Allan, McEachrane
Scorers:- McKay, Carnelly, Joyce

24. 01. 1900 Gravesend (A) 1-2
1200
Moore, Dunn, King, Bigden, Stewart, Craig, Allan, McKay, Joyce, Carnelly, McEachrane
Scorer:- Carnelly

10. 02. 1900 Bedminster (A) 1-3
2000
Moore, Dunn, King, Craig, Stewart, McEachrane, Allan, McKay, Joyce, Carnelly, Taylor
Scorer:- Carnelly

17. 02. 1900 Bristol Rovers (H) 0-0
4000
Moore, Dunn, King, Dove, Stewart, McEachrane, Allan, McKay, Joyce, Carnelly, Taylor

24. 02. 1900 Portsmouth (A) 0-2
2000
Moore, Dunn, King, Bigden, Stewart, McEachrane, Allan, McKay, Joyce, Carnelly, Taylor

10. 03. 1900 Tottenham Hotspur (H) 0-0
9000
Moore, Dunn, King, Dove, Stewart, McEachrane, Allan, McKay, Joyce, Carnelly, Taylor

17. 03. 1900 New Brompton (A) 1-3
2000
Moore, Dunn, Gilmore, Bigden, Stewart, McEachrane, Allan, McKay, Joyce, Carnelly, Taylor
Scorer:- 1 O. G.

24. 03. 1900 Gravesend (H) 2-1
3500
Moore, Dunn, Turner, Allan, Stewart, McEachrane, Janes, McKay, Joyce, Carnelly, Taylor
Scorer:- Carnelly 2

31. 03. 1900 Swindon Town (A) 1-3
3000
Moore, Dunn, Craig, Dove, Stewart, McEachrane, Allan, McKay, Joyce, Carnelly, Taylor
Scorer:- 1 O. G

05. 04. 1900 Portsmouth (H) 2-4
5000
Moore, Dunn, Craig, Dove, Stewart, McEachrane, Allan, McKay, Joyce, Carnelly, Taylor
Scorer:-Joyce 2

07. 04. 1900 Bristol City (H) 0-0
5000
Moore, Dunn, Craig, Dove, Stewart, McEachrane, Allan, McKay, Joyce, Carnelly, Taylor

09. 04. 1900 Southampton (H) 4-1
4000
Moore, Dunn, Craig, Dove, Stewart, McEachrane, Allan, McKay, Joyce, Carnelly, Taylor
Scorers:- Joyce 3, Allan

17. 04. 1900 Sheppey Utd (H) 4-2
3000
Moore, Dunn, Craig, Dove, Stewart, McEachrane, Allan, McKay, Joyce, Carnelly, Taylor
Scorers:- McKay, Joyce, Taylor, 1 O. G.

28. 04. 1900 Millwall (A) 1-0
8000
Moore, Dunn, Craig, Dove, Stewart, McEachrane, Allan, McKay, Joyce, Carnelly, Taylor
Scorer:- McKay

Test Match (play off) 1899/1900
(played at Tottenham)
30. 04. 1900 Fulham   5-1
600
Moore, Dunn, Craig, Dove, Stewart, McEachrane,
Allan, McKay, Joyce, Carnelly, Taylor
Scorers;- Joyce 3, Stewart, 1 O. G.

Southern League Division One
Final Table 1899-1900

	P	W	D	L	F	A	Pts
Tottenham Hotspur	28	20	4	4	67	26	44
Portsmouth	28	20	1	7	59	29	41
Southampton	28	17	1	10	70	33	35
Reading	28	15	2	11	41	28	32
Swindon Town	28	15	2	11	50	42	32
Bedminster	28	13	2	13	44	45	28
Millwall	28	12	3	13	36	37	27
Queen's Park Rangers	28	12	2	14	50	58	26
Bristol City	28	9	7	12	44	47	25
Bristol Rovers	28	11	3	14	46	55	25
New Brompton	28	9	6	13	39	49	24
Gravesend United	28	10	4	14	38	58	24
Chatham	28	10	3	15	38	58	23
Thames Ironworks	28	8	5	15	30	45	21
Sheppey United	28	3	7	18	24	66	13

Players appearances:- (including Test Match)
Roddy McEachrane 29, Kenny McKay 29, Albert
Carnelly 28, Bill Joyce 28, Tommy Moore 28,
Robert Allan 22, Tommy Dunn 22, Charlie Craig
18, William Stewart 17, Charlie Dove 16, Syd King
16, Frank Taylor 15, James Bigden 11, L. Walker
7, F. Adams 6, 'Harry' Bradshaw 5, Peter
McManus 5, Henry Gilmore 4, Turner 4, Fred
Corbett 3, W. Janes 2, Gentle 1, Henry Hird 1,
James Reid 1, H. Sunderland 1

Goal Scorers:- (including Test Match) Joyce 11,
Carnelly 8, McKay 8, Adams 1, Allan 1, Stewart 1,
Taylor 1, O. G.'s 4

F.A. Cup 1899/1900

23. 09. 1899 Royal Engineers   (H)   6-0
1000
Moore, Dunn, King Dove, McManus,
McEachrane, Hird, McKay, Joyce, J Reid,
Bradshaw
Scorers:- Joyce 3, McKay, McEachrane, Reid

30. 09. 1899 Grays Utd   (A)   4-0
750
Moore, Dunn, King, Dove, McManus,
McEachrane, Hird, McKay, Joyce, Carnelly,
Bradshaw
Scorers:- Joyce, McKay, Carnelly, McManus

14. 10. 1899 Sheppey Utd   (H)   4-2
2000
Moore, Dunn, King, Dove, McManus,
McEachrane, Hird, McKay, Joyce, Carnelly,
Bradshaw
Scorers:- Carnelly 2, Joyce 2

28. 10. 1899 Dartford   (A)   7-0
1200
Moore, Dunn, King, Dove, McManus,
McEachrane, Craig, McKay, Joyce, Carnelly,
Bradshaw
Scorers:- Carnelly 2, McKay 2, Joyce,
McEachrane, Bradshaw

18. 11. 1899 New Brompton   (A)   0-0
3000
Moore, Dunn, King, Craig, Bigden, McEachrane,
Gentle, McKay, Joyce, Carnelly, Bradshaw

23. 11. 1899 NewBrompton   (H)   2-0
3000
Moore, Dunn, King, Craig, Bigden, McEachrane,
Adams, McKay, Joyce, Carnelly, Bradshaw
Scorers:- Carnelly, McKay

09. 12. 1899 Millwall   (H)   1-2
13000
Moore, Dunn, King, Craig, Dove, McEachrane,
Adams, McKay, Joyce, Carnelly, Bradshaw
Scorer:-Bradshaw

Thames & Medway Combination 1899/1900

24. 10. 1899 Sheppey Utd   (A)   3-3
Moore, Dunn, King, Dove, McManus,
McEachrane, Craig, McKay, Joyce, Carnelly,
Bradshaw
Scorers:- McKay 1 + 1 pen, Carnelly

30. 10. 1899 Chatham   (A)   1-1
Moore, Dunn, King, Dove, McManus,
McEachrane, Craig, McKay, Joyce, Carnelly,
Bradshaw
 Scorer:- Bradshaw

06. 11. 1899 Grays Utd   (H)   11-1
Sunderland, Grelby, King, Hird, Rose,
McEachrane, Janes, McKay, Carnelly, J Reid,
Bradshaw
Scorers:- Bradshaw 5, Carnelly 4, J Reid 2

11. 12. 1899 New Brompton   (A)   0-2
Moore, Craig, King, Dove, Bigden, McEachrane,
Allan, McKay, Joyce, Carnelly, Walker

26. 12. 1899 Gravesend   (H)   0-0
Moore, Craig, Adams, Gilmore, Bigden,
McEachrane, Allan, McKay, Joyce, Carnelly,
Walker

12. 02. 1900 New Brompton   (H)   1-1
Moore, Dunn, King, Craig, Stewart, Dove,
Allan, McKay, Joyce, Carnelly, Taylor
Scorer:- Joyce

01. 03. 1900 Sheppey Utd   (II)   5-1
Moore, Dunn, King, McManus, Stewart,
McEachrane, Allan, McKay, Joyce, Carnelly,
Taylor
Scorers:- Taylor 2, McKay, Carnelly, Joyce

21. 3. 1900 Grays Utd   (A)   0-0
McKay, Dunn, Yenson, Janes, Stewart,
McEachrane, Allan, Corbett, Joyce, Carnelly,
Taylor

29. 03. 1900 Chatham   (H)   2-2
Moore, Dunn, Turner, Dove, Stewart,
McEachrane, Allan, McKay, Joyce, Carnelly,
Taylor
Scorers:- Joyce, McKay

16. 04. 1900 Gravesend   (A)   1-1
Moore, Dunn, Craig, Dove, Stewart, McEachrane,
Allan, McKay, Joyce, Carnelly, Taylor
Scorer:- Craig

Thames & Medway Combination Final Table 1899-1900

	P	W	D	L	F	A	Pts
New Brompton	10	8	1	1	20	6	17
Chatham	10	5	3	2	22	12	13
Thames Ironworks	10	2	7	1	24	12	11
Gravesend	10	4	3	3	15	13	11
Sheppey United	10	1	2	7	10	24	4
Grays United	10	1	2	7	7	31	4

Player appearances:- Albert Carnelly 10, Kenny
McKay 10, William Joyce 9, Roddy McEachrane
9, Tommy Moore 8, Robert Allan 7, Tommy Dunn
7, Charlie Craig 6, Charlie Dove 6, Syd King 6,
William Stewart 5, Frank Taylor 5, 'Harry'
Bradshaw 3, Peter McManus 3, James Bigden 2,
Janes 2, J. Walker 2, F. Adams 1, Fred Corbett 1,
Henry Gilmore 1, Grelby 1, Henry Hird 1, James
Reid 1, Rose 1, H. Sunderland 1, Turner 1, Yenson
1

Goal Scorers:- Bradshaw 6, Carnelly 6, McKay 4,
Joyce 3, J Reid 2, Taylor 2, Craig 1

Friendly matches 1899/1900

13. 11. 1899	Luton Town	(H)	2-0
03. 02. 1900	Chatham	(H)	1-0
03. 03. 1900	Clapton	(H)	2-1
13. 04. 1900	Rushden	(H)	3-0

Thames Ironworks Reserves
London League 1899-1900

23/09/1899	Millwall Res	A		0-1
21/10/1899	Barnet	A		1-3
04/11/1899	Tottenham Res	H		1-3
09/12/1899	Clapton Orient	A		0-0
16/12/1899	QPR Res	H		1-2
30/12/1899	Hammersmith Ath	A		1-2
06/01/1900	Willesden Town	H		3-1
13/01/1900	QPR Res	A		0-1
20/01/1900	Hammersmith Ath	H		4-1
27/01/1900	Monsteds Ath	H		4-1
24/02/1900	Clapton Orient	H		6-0
03/03/1900	Barnet	H		5-2
10/03/1900	Tottenham Res	A		2-2
17/03/1900	Millwall Res	H		3-2
19/03/1900	Monsteds Ath	A		2-1
24/03/1900	Willesden Town	A		5-1
16/04/1900	Commercial Ath	H		2-0
28/04/1900	Commercial Ath	A		2-0

London League Final Table 1899-1900

	P	W	D	L	F	A	Pts
Millwall Res	18	16	0	2	70	15	32
Tottenham H Res *	18	14	2	2	74	24	28
QPR Res	18	12	1	5	40	20	25
Thames Ironworks Res	18	10	2	6	42	23	22
Monsteds Ath.	18	10	0	8	42	42	20
Clapton Orient	18	4	5	9	40	50	13
Commercial Ath.	18	4	3	11	24	42	11
Willesdon Town	18	5	1	12	27	66	11
Barnet	18	4	2	12	33	52	10
Hammersmith Ath.	18	3	0	15	13	71	6

Deducted two points for playing an ineligible player

*The majority of full line-ups for the reserve team
are not available. Sunderland played most
fixtures in goal, whilst Yenson, Turner, Gentle,
Bigden, Barker and Gilmore figured more often
that not in defence and midfield. The forwards
were very ably served by Foss, Corbett,
Hitchens, Thompson and Walker, with Corbett
being a prolific top scorer. First team men were
occasionally called upon including the complete
forward line and Dove and McManus also made
appearances.*

EPILOGUE

Before the new season of 1900/01 began the sports correspondent of the 'West Ham Guardian' gave a preview of the new club and an impassioned plea: *Today the West Ham United F. C. is in the hands of you locals. It is your club, and you, who are shareholders, have a voice in its management. Those who are not, I make a strenuous appeal to all for support. It would be a standing disgrace to a district like West Ham, which is considered a hot-bed of football, if the club were allowed to go unsupported. I have the names of the players before me, and I see no reason why we should not figure high up in the Southern League table. In closing, I would say, let there be unity of action. Let each supporter strive for the good of his club both on and off the field. Let each work for one end—that of making the club the best in England. Much depends on a good rousing cheer when things are going against your side. Be liberal with your praise and sparing with your criticism. Above all, be sportsmen and gentlemen. Success and failure hang in the balance. Everything depends upon on you. Will you make the club a success? And as a sportsman I think – dropping the third person for a moment – the answer is 'We will'.*

By March 1901 there were still 260 shares left to be sold in the new club. At 10 shillings each they could be purchased in four instalments of 2/6d each.

In addition to the fact that Arnold Hills was the major shareholder in the new club and had granted use of the Memorial Grounds for the club for three years, the Thames Ironworks Gazette still continued to report the club's affairs (as West Ham United) in 1901/02. There was mention of 'our teams' in respect of the first and second XIs. In the 'Gazette' of September 1901 it was stated that '*...we have upholstered about sixty seats in our grandstand for those of our supporters who wish to make sure of a comfortable sitting at every match.*'

By the beginning of 1902/03 however, enthusiasm at Thames was drifting off. Mention was just made that '*although the WHU club is now governed by an Independent Board of Directors, as its parents we are interested from time to time......*'

Although Thames Ironworks FC was no more, a new club arose in the Works under the name of Thames Ironworks Alliance. In 1901/02 they entered the West Ham Charity cup competition and in 1904 they were members of the Eastern Suburban League. Within the Works itself a football competition was organised called the Trades Challenge Shield. This resulted in such clashes as Fitters v Engineers, Staff v Platers, Caulkers v Shipwrights and Blacksmiths v Electricians. It was first played for in 1900/01 and the winners were the Platers who beat the Labourers 4-0.

In 1904 the ex-club secretary Lew Bowen confirmed rumours that West Ham United were to move to the grounds of the Boleyn Castle at Upton Park. In that respect he stated: 'We wish them success on their new ground and when in their hour of triumph, should they perchance to look back at old days, we hope that they will not forget their parents—the Thames Ironworks FC—and when I think of that club familiar faces come before me, faces of those who now occupy places of honour in the football world.'

It has often been said that the nickname of West Ham United is the 'Hammers', in fact the present day match programme carries that title and press reports often refer to the club as such, but listen to the chants both at Upton Park and at away matches, and remembering the pioneering days of the Ironworks club the call is always 'COME ON YOU IRONS!'

The Thames Ironworks site today. The main office building and docks were off-picture, just to the photographer's right. The scrubland in the middle distance was the site of the main slipways.

Now a steel stockholder's premises, but once the entrance to the Ironwork's dock in front of the main office building.

Foremen at the Yard. The man at the left of the middle row, fingers in waistcoat pocket, is George Dove, the father of Charlie.

The Memorial Grounds in 2005. The pavilion once stood on the left of this photograph, at the end of Memorial Avenue. The far side of the ground bordered the East London Cemetery, the fence of which is just visible on the right.

BIBLIOGRAPHY

Association Football and The Men Who Made It Vols 1-4, Alfred Gibson And William Pickford, Caxton Publishing 1907

The Book of Football, The Amalgamated Press Ltd, London 1906

Football League Players' Records 1888-1939, Michael Joyce, SoccerData, 2002

Founded on Iron, Brian Belton, Tempus Publishing Ltd 2003

Fulham Facts and Figures 1879-1998, Dennis Turner and Alex White, Northdown Publishing Limited 1998

The Southern League First Division 1894-1920, AFS Publications 1984

West Ham United A Complete Record, John Northcutt & Roy Shoesmith, Breedon Books 1993

West Ham United by Charles Korr, Gerald Duckworth & Co. Ltd 1986

The Definitive West Ham United, John Northcutt, SoccerData 2003

Newspapers and Periodicals:-
Thames Ironworks Gazette 1895-1905
Borough of West Ham and Stratford Express 1887-1894
Borough of West Ham, East Ham and Stratford Express 1894-1901
West Ham Herald and South Essex Gazette 1892-1899
County Borough of West Ham Guardian 1898-1902
The Football Chat and Athletic World 1904
The Football Sun 1899
The Sportsman 1895-1900
Athletic News
Plus a large number of provincial newspapers of the period

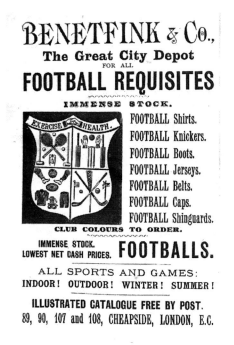

INDEX TO PLAYER PROFILES

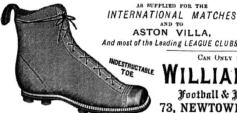